MARK W. FOREMAN

PRELUDE TO PHILOSOPHY

AN INTRODUCTION FOR CHRISTIANS

IVP Academic

An imprint of InterVarsity Press
Downers Grove, Illinois

InterVarsity Press
P.O. Box 1400, Downers Grove, IL 60515-1426
World Wide Web: www.ivpress.com
Email: email@ivpress.com

©2014 by Mark W. Foreman

InterVarsity Press® is the book-publishing division of InterVarsity Christian Fellowship/USA®, a movement of students and faculty active on campus at hundreds of universities, colleges and schools of nursing in the United States of America, and a member movement of the International Fellowship of Evangelical Students. For information about local and regional activities, write Public Relations Dept., InterVarsity Christian Fellowship/USA, 6400 Schroeder Rd., P.O. Box 7895, Madison, WI 53707-7895, or visit the IVCF website at www.intervarsity.org.

All Scripture quotations, unless otherwise indicated, are taken from the New American Standard Bible®, copyright 1960, 1962, 1963, 1968, 1971, 1972, 1973, 1975, 1977, 1995 by The Lockman Foundation. Used by permission.

While all stories in this book are true, some names and identifying information in this book have been changed to protect the privacy of the individuals involved.

Cover design: David Fassett
Interior design: Beth Hagenberg
Image: ©Igor Djurovic/iStockphoto

ISBN 978-0-8308-3960-5 (print)
ISBN 978-0-8308-6995-4 (digital)

Printed in the United States of America ∞

green press INITIATIVE

InterVarsity Press is committed to protecting the environment and to the responsible use of natural resources. As a member of Green Press Initiative we use recycled paper whenever possible. To learn more about the Green Press Initiative, visit www.greenpressinitiative.org.

Library of Congress Cataloging-in-Publication Data

Foreman, Mark W. (Mark Wesley), 1954-
Prelude to philosophy : an introduction for Christians / Mark W. Foreman.
       pages cm
Includes bibliographical references and index.
ISBN 978-0-8308-3960-5 (pbk. : alk. paper)
1. Christian philosophy. 2. Philosophy—Introductions. I. Title.
BR100.F655 2014
102'.427—dc23
                                                                2013040766

P 20 19 18 17 16 15 14 13 12 11 10 9 8 7 6 5
Y 31 30 29 28 27 26 25 24 23 22 21 20 19 18 17 16 15 14

Dedicated to the memory of

Scott Earl Foreman

Paul Stanley Foreman

Patrick Philip ("Flip") Foreman

CONTENTS

FOREWORD

Although 1974 was declared the year of the evangelical, apparently no one was listening. The year came and went as our culture continued slouching toward Gomorrah. Fast-forward to 2013. Islamic terrorism threatens our borders, our political discourse is shrill, and an epidemic of pornography addiction threatens the possibility of healthy relationships between men and women. People have to think twice about whether saving aborted babies or snail darters is more important. We cannot agree about the sexual makeup of a flourishing family. Spirituality is in, but no one knows which form to embrace. Indeed, the idea that one form may be better than another seems arrogant and intolerant. A flat stomach is of greater value than a mature character. The makeup man is more important than the speechwriter. People listen, or pretend to listen, to what actors—*actors!*—have to say. Western Civ had to go, and along with it, the possibility of getting a robust university education. The content of public discourse can be communicated in thirty-second sound bites. Magazine and newspaper articles are written at what used to be an eighth-grade level.

A moment's reflection on these issues awakens us to the fact that our culture is in deep trouble. And while the causes of our malaise are varied, a core problem is the general inability of the American people to think carefully about things that really matter. And the church of Jesus Christ, which is called to be the pillar and support of the truth, is just as anti-intellectual as the broader culture. There is a straightforward application of the church's anti-intellectualism for the body of Christ's ability to affect the world for Jesus. To see this, consider the fact that a person's plausibility structure is the set of ideas the person either is or is not willing to entertain as possibly true. For example, no one would come to a lecture defending a flat earth because this idea is not part of our plausibility structure. We cannot even entertain the idea. Moreover, a person's plausibility structure is a function of the beliefs he or she already has. Applied to outreach, J. Gresham Machen got it right when he said:

God usually exerts that power in connection with certain prior conditions of the human mind, and it should be ours to create, so far as we can, with the help of God, those favourable conditions for the reception of the gospel. False ideas are the greatest obstacles to the reception of the gospel. We may preach with all the fervour of a reformer and yet succeed only in winning a straggler here and there, if we permit the whole collective thought of the nation or of the world to be controlled by ideas which, by the resistless force of logic, prevent Christianity from being regarded as anything more than a harmless delusion.[1]

If a culture reaches the point where Christian claims are not even part of its plausibility structure, fewer and fewer people will be able to entertain the possibility that they might be true. Whatever stragglers do come to faith in such a context would do so on the basis of felt needs alone, and the genuineness of such conversions would be questionable. This is why a vibrant intellectual life is so crucial to evangelism. It empowers the church to be able to create a plausibility structure in a person's mind, "favourable conditions" as Machen puts it, so the gospel can be entertained by that person. To plant a seed in someone's mind in pre-evangelism is to present a person with an idea that will work on his or her plausibility structure to create a space in which Christianity can be entertained seriously. If this is important to evangelism, it is strategically crucial that local churches think about how they can address those aspects of the modern worldview that place Christianity outside the plausibility structures of so many.

[1]J. Gresham Machen, address delivered on September 20, 1912, at the opening of the 101st session of Princeton Theological Seminary.

It is at this point that training in philosophy and logic enters the picture. Training in philosophy can empower someone to think well about life's most important questions, to pursue thoughtfully a life of wisdom and virtue and to foster a plausibility structure in the broader culture within which Christian truth claims will be taken seriously. One of the chief omissions in education from elementary school to college is the lack of training in philosophy. And it is this omission that *Prelude to Philosophy* solves. I have known Mark Foreman for more than a quarter of a century. He is a man of integrity, vast and deep learning, and wide experience in teaching and writing. With great skill, he leads the reader to a feast of ideas, a journey into argumentation and thought, a pilgrimage into discipleship of the mind. This is one of the most accessible books of its kind, and the reader will be delighted by the clarity of exposition and the rich use of illustrations. So get ready for an adventure in thought and an invitation to love your God with all of your mind.

J. P. Moreland

PREFACE

This book is called *Prelude to Philosophy: An Introduction for Christians*. A prelude may be defined as an introduction preceding and preparing for a principal or more important matter. That is the sense in which this book is an introduction to philosophy. Most introductory texts present a quick definition of philosophy, contain a paragraph or two on why its study is important and spend the bulk of the book delving into the major branches, issues and problems in philosophy. This book takes a different approach. It concentrates on what philosophy is, why it is important and how to go about doing it. Little space is devoted to examining specific philosophical issues. This is a prolegomenon to philosophy. As such, it was written primarily to be used as a supplementary text for the beginning of an introduction to philosophy course.

Another distinction of this book is that it was written for a specific audience: Christians who are new to philosophy and who may have misgivings and reservations about what they are getting into. It is written at a basic level and assumes the reader has no knowledge of philosophy. It is hoped that reading this book will encourage Christians to continue to develop a philosophical mindset and be better prepared to consider the issues and problems in philosophy.

The layout of the book is straightforward. Chapter one covers the basics of defining and describing philosophy. In chapters two and three we take up the question of why the study of philosophy is important.

Chapter two discusses why developing a philosophical mindset is important in general, and chapter three discusses why it is vital specifically for Christians. Chapter four offers an overview of the different branches and major questions dealt with in philosophy. The last three chapters deal with the primary method of philosophy: logic and analysis of arguments. Chapter five introduces the reader to the basic language and types of logical reasoning, chapter six covers informal fallacies, and chapter seven offers a tactical approach to constructing and analyzing arguments. The book finishes with an epilogue on the virtues of the Christian philosopher.

The book would not have been possible without the support of many friends and colleagues. First, there are of those former teachers who have had a significant influence on my approach to philosophy and whose shadows will be seen in these pages: Dr. Norman Geisler, Dr. Gary Habermas and Dr. James F. Childress. I want to thank my colleagues in the philosophy department at Liberty University with whom I shared many of these ideas. I especially want to thank my good friend and fellow teacher Dr. David Baggett, who read every page of this work and offered many valuable suggestions that improved it considerably. Also I offer a big thank you to my friend and mentor Dr. J. P. Moreland for his constant advice and encouragement and for writing the foreword to this book. As always, I could not get anything accomplished without the tireless devotion of my wife, Chris, and my three daughters, Erin, Lindsay and Kelly. Finally, I want to dedicate this volume to my three brothers who passed away during my work on it. They live on daily in my memory.

one

WHAT IS PHILOSOPHY?

I have been teaching a course on the introduction of philosophy on the college level every semester for about twenty years. In my experience, the initial attitude most students have about taking my class is one of dread. I am fully aware that I face an uphill battle if I am going to win them over to becoming even remotely interested, let alone excited, about studying philosophy. Why do most new students have such a negative attitude? To discover why, I often play a word association game with my students on the first day of class. I say the word *philosophy* and they have to tell me the first thing that comes into their minds. Here are some of their responses: "heavy," "super-smart," "complex," "confusing," "unimportant," "dull," "impractical," "ivory-tower minded," and the paradigmatically inevitable "boring."[1] There is no doubt about it: philosophy has a major public relations problem.

It is not only novices who have such a low regard for philosophy. Well-known, intelligent writers and thinkers have not uncommonly held philosophy in low regard too. Historian Henry Adams referred to philosophy as "unintelligible answers to insoluble problems." Lord Bowen, a British statesman and writer, commented that a philosopher is "a blind man in a dark room looking for a black cat that isn't there." The nineteenth-century American satirist Ambrose Pierce defined phi-

---

[1] A few students also say complimentary things. But why share those responses? It would spoil my point.

losophy as "a route of many roads leading from nowhere to nothing." Even philosophers themselves have made disparaging remarks about their craft. Cicero wrote, "There is nothing so absurd that it hasn't been said by some philosopher." American philosopher William James claimed, "There is only one thing a philosopher can be relied on to do, and that is to contradict other philosophers." French philosopher René Descartes wrote that "one cannot conceive of anything so strange and so unbelievable that it has not been said by one philosopher or another." And he is considered the father of modern philosophy! Bertrand Russell once wrote, "The point of philosophy is to start with something so simple as to seem not worth stating, and to end with something so paradoxical that no one will believe it." Finally, there is the well-known description of a philosopher: someone who doesn't know what he is talking about but makes it sound like it's your fault.

Returning to my students, what is the reason for such a low view among new students who have never studied philosophy? There are a number of factors. Partly it has to do with the image that one has to be superintelligent to do philosophy. However, that is not true. Certainly a high intelligence level will help in philosophical investigation. But philosophy is more about rigor and hard work than natural intelligence. Most philosophical thinking can be done by the average person if he or she is willing to put in the time and effort. However, much of this modern generation has become intellectually lazy. Many of them let others, such as teachers, pastors and the media, do the hard work of researching and thinking through tough issues and then rely on them to dictate what to believe. I often lecture on opposing views of a particular ethical issue in class, and it still amazes me when a student will raise her hand and ask, "So what do I believe?"

Another reason for philosophy's bad image is that, as a discipline, most students study it late in their academic development. Most courses taken in college are built on material studied in high school or elementary school, like math, history and biology. Students have a basic idea of what these subjects cover before they walk through the doors of a college. However, most students do not take their first philosophy course until after they get to college. This perpetuates the myth that philosophy is only for the academically elite. But the fact is that people begin to think philosophically when they are young children. David Baggett recently made this point in *Harry Potter and Philosophy*:

"Philosophy begins in wonder," Plato said. The mystery and marvel of it all is rarely lost on a child. Youngsters don't need to be taught philosophical curiosity. It just comes naturally. Nearly as soon as we learn to talk, the world and its mysteries enchant our imagination. Who am I? Why are we here? Who made God? Does the refrigerator light go off when we close the door? Kids are born philosophers. Usually only the concerted efforts of adults—understandably exasperated at answering "Why?"—can stifle children's passion to understand.[2]

It seems at a certain point children lose that sense of wonder for a while, but it often returns around the time of adolescence when they begin to question what they have been taught all their lives to believe. That is why I am a strong advocate for offering high-school courses in philosophy. This is the perfect time to channel the questions they are asking into a formal course on philosophy. I taught philosophy at the high-school level for a number of years, and it was exciting to watch students consider the views of the classic philosophers and marvel at how these philosophers struggled with many of the same questions that people face today.

Another reason for philosophy's bad image is that most people do not think it is practical. Their impression is that philosophy is something done in the ivory towers of academia, and it has no place on Main Street where the common Joe is just trying to get by and live his life. To be honest, part of the blame for this perception has to be placed on philosophers themselves. Sometimes students do get the idea that certain ideas and concepts taught in the academy are highly impractical outside the classroom. Most philosophical concepts and issues are not like that, however. As the next chapter will show, philosophy is practical and beneficial. Our everyday decisions are based on our overall philosophy of life. Therefore, it is important that we take the time to examine those

[2]David Baggett, "The Magic of Philosophy," in *Harry Potter and Philosophy: If Aristotle Ran Hogwarts*, ed. David Baggett and Shawn E. Klein (Chicago: Open Court, 2004), p. 2.

background foundational beliefs to make sure we are headed down the right path in life.[3]

However, the main reason new students have such a negative attitude about philosophy is that they do not know what it is or how it can benefit them. That is the purpose of the first three chapters of this book. This chapter will discuss what philosophy is, and the next two will discuss its benefits. What is philosophy? Four ways to get to know what something is are the following: define it, describe it, contrast and compare it with similar things, and experience it. Let us look at each of these in regards to philosophy.

PHILOSOPHY: A WORKING DEFINITION

The attempt to define philosophy brings us face to face with our first philosophical controversy. Philosophers cannot seem to come to an agreement about exactly what philosophy is. The problem is that the term is so broad and encompasses so many areas that it is difficult to arrive at an exact designation of what it means. It is like defining "love" or "good." It is tough to get a specific handle on it because people mean so many things when they use these ambiguous terms.

Part of the confusion is that "philosophy" can be used as a noun or with a verb. As a noun it often refers to a person's point of view on a particular topic. When I was once being interviewed for a teaching position, I was asked, "What is your philosophy of education?" The interviewers were asking me for a set of beliefs I had about the nature of education and the process for accomplishing it. That is one way to think of philosophy. However, the term can also function as a verb or an activity. To *do* philosophy is to *practice* a particular kind of mental activity. That is the operational definition I am seeking here.

Perhaps a good place to start is by looking at what a famous philosopher said about philosophy. Almost everyone has heard of Socrates. Socrates lived in ancient Greece from 469 to 399 B.C. He was originally a stonemason who, according to legend, was told by the Oracle of Delphi

---

[3]By showing how philosophy is practical I am not confirming the message that only the practical has value. In fact, I think the rampant and narrow pragmatism that dominates our culture has caused more harm than good. This is especially the case in our approach toward education.

that he was the wisest man alive.[4] Finding this difficult to believe, he set off to find someone wiser than himself. Socrates engaged several of the statesmen and poets of Athens in dialogues about the ultimate meaning of things. His tactic was to corner an individual and barrage him with questions about what he was doing, why he was doing it and its ultimate meaning. In almost all of these dialogues, he showed the individual how ignorant he was concerning these questions.[5] This earned Socrates the reputation of being a fairly annoying individual, and he became known as the Gadfly of Athens. Eventually, he became so irritating that the citizens of Athens put him on trial on the trumped-up charges of not honoring the gods and of corrupting the youth.

During his trial, Socrates gave a stirring defense for living the life of a philosopher in which he claimed, "The unexamined life is not worth living." What did Socrates mean? Specifically, what is the unexamined life and what did Socrates mean when he said it was not worth living?

Socrates often ran into individuals who were immersed in the daily activities of life, who rarely took time to stop and think about what they were doing and why they were doing it. They were going through the motions of life without making the effort to reflect and think about what life is about. That is the unexamined life. Many today are guilty of living much the same way. They perform activities or make choices without reflecting about the kind of life they live or where they are going. Oftentimes they adopt beliefs without thinking about them.

I once had a conversation with a friend about morality, in the course of which he told me, "I think that everything is okay to do as long as you are not hurting anyone." As we talked, I asked him if he thought such a minimal view of morality was adequate. I offered the following scenario: "Suppose I am standing next to a shallow swimming pool. A toddler crawls over and falls into the pool and starts drowning. It would be no trouble for me to reach down and pull her out of the water. And yet I do nothing and allow her to drown. Do you think I am doing something

---

[4]In Greek mythology the Oracle of Delphi was a spokesperson for the god Apollo.
[5]For the sake of full disclosure, Socrates's questions were often very hard to answer, but rather than acknowledge this, his interlocutors claimed to have a good grasp of the answer until they were shown otherwise.

wrong?" He said, "Absolutely! You should save the child." I then replied, "But if your minimalistic view of morality is true, I am not obligated to save this child. I am not hurting the child—I didn't push her in, she just fell in. According to your moral theory, I can do anything I want as long as I am not hurting someone. So, I am free to stand there doing nothing, and I am not culpable of any wrongdoing." My friend acknowledged that he needed to qualify his view. He realized that morality often involves more than refraining from harming others. It also involves other obligations, such as sometimes helping others as well. He had thoughtlessly adopted a common cliché about morality without examining what it means and whether it is true. That is typical of living the unexamined life.

What does Socrates mean when he says that such a life is not worth living? He does not mean it in the absolute sense—that people have no value if they live unexamined lives. Neither is Socrates saying that people who do not examine their lives should be executed. One can gain a better grasp of Socrates' claim by putting it in context. In his defense, Socrates suggests some of his accusers might ask, "Why can't you live quietly and stop talking?" To which he answers, "It is the greatest good for a man to discuss virtue every day and those other things about which you hear me conversing and testing myself and others for the unexamined life is not worth living for man."[6]

Socrates sees human beings as unique in the animal kingdom. Human beings have, by nature of the kind of being they are, the inherent ability to reason and reflect about themselves and the world around them.[7]

For example, when I take my dog, Toby, for a walk in the evening, I often stop and look at the view of the sunset behind the Blue Ridge Mountains that I see from my neighborhood. I admire the beauty of God's world and wonder at his majesty. Toby is not having any kind of

[6]Plato, *Apology*, in *Classics of Western Philosophy*, ed. Stephen M. Cahn, trans. G. M. A. Grube, 3rd ed. (Indianapolis: Hackett, 1977) p. 54.

[7]This is not to say that other animals may not have certain cognitive abilities. However, they do not seem to have the deeper capacities for rational reflection and willful deliberation. They might have beliefs, but they do not seem to have beliefs about their beliefs. By saying humans have this ability inherently, I mean they have it by nature of the kind of being they are. This would extend to all human beings, including the unborn, the mentally handicapped and those who are comatose. Although they might not be able to express their ability to reason or reflect, they have this inherent ability by nature of being human.

similar experience—he is looking for a spot to relieve himself. Toby does not have the ability to reflect on the beauty of the world, but human beings do. It was Jean-Paul Sartre, a French existentialist philosopher, who said that the human animal is the only animal that knows it is going to die. That knowledge affects us even when we are not consciously thinking about our own mortality. We plan our days knowing that our time is limited. We can and often do think about things like God, the afterlife, morality and the meaning of our existence in light of the fact that we will at some point shuffle off this mortal coil and be buried in the cold, dark earth. Toby does not think about that. He is not going to wake up one day and suddenly think, "My Lord, what have I been doing with my life? My life is passing before me, and all I do is lie around all day and chew up the furniture. Is that all there is?" When Socrates claims that the unexamined life is not worth living, he is saying that we are not living the life we were created to live. To live the unexamined life is to live a less than fully human life. It is like living the life of a lower animal, like a dog or a cow. It is not the way humans were made to live. Human beings are designed to be able to reflect on the meaning and value of life and the world around them.

This is what Socrates means when he claims, "The unexamined life is not worth living." But that raises another question: Is this claim true? Just because Socrates claims that the unexamined life is not worth living does not automatically make it true. Maybe that is just his opinion. [8] After all, many people seem to be happy, and they do not seem to take the time to examine their lives. In fact, some people might argue that it is better not to know everything. There is a certain amount of truth to the cliché, "Ignorance is bliss."

To answer the truth question, it is important to see that Socrates is making a normative claim. A normative claim makes a claim about

---

[8]Often when individuals either do not want to or cannot discuss or debate a point, they punt to this little phrase ("It's *just* your opinion") as a way of shutting down the conversation. However, in this context rarely is a philosophical argument *just* some philosopher's opinion. I am not denying that there is not a certain subjective element involved, but it is usually a well-thought-out and well-reasoned idea worthy of investigation. It is not on the level of a personal preference like a favorite flavor of ice cream. A well-thought-out and argued claim deserves more serious evaluation than a dismissive "That's *just* your opinion."

some action persons ought to do. When someone says you should not lie or you should help your fellow human, she is making a normative claim. Socrates is not just saying that because a person is a rational creature, that person has an obligation to behave like one. When one lives the "unexamined life," one is not living as one should. The "greatest good" is examining life. Socrates would ask the person who is supposedly happy living the unexamined life, "Is happiness really *all* that matters? What about the truth? What if an individual is happy, yet everything he believes is wrong?"

Take the story about Wonmug.[9] Wonmug was not a smart person; in fact, he was very slow on the upswing. One day, several of the students in his class decided to play a cruel hoax on Wonmug. They were going to act as if everything he said was intelligent. Every time Wonmug made a remark or answered a question, even though he was wrong, they made comments like, "That was very insightful, Wonmug," and "You are really smart, Wonmug." So, while the class was laughing behind his back, Wonmug was happy because he thought he was smart. How many of us would want to be Wonmug? Could one be satisfied living a happy life that may be a delusion? Might one be forfeiting a deeper sense of fulfillment by settling for a poor substitute? Socrates would doubt that any such person could ultimately be happy. Human beings are creatures who want to know and understand the truth about themselves and the world around them. Many would even be willing to sacrifice some temporary happiness for timeless knowledge and truth.[10] It is the way people are and the way they should be.

So, what is philosophy? Broadly speaking, it is examining life. However, that is a rather expansive definition, so let us narrow it down. A second way to define philosophy is by examining the etymology of the word.[11] *Philosophy* is the combination of two terms in Greek: *phileo* and *sophos. Phileo* is a term for "love." The Greeks had many terms for

[9] I do not know the origin of the story of Wonmug. I first heard it from J. P. Moreland.

[10] Christians know that ultimate happiness is not at odds with truth. Jesus said the truth will set us free. The three things Christians strive after our whole lives—truth, beauty and goodness—ultimately all come together in the beatific vision.

[11] Etymology is the study of the origin and historical development of words.

the idea that we communicate with the single word *love*. The English term *love* can have several different meanings: a romantic feeling as in "I love you," a commitment like "love of country," an expression of joy as in "I love this song." In Greek, each nuance of "love" has a different term. *Phileo* is usually meant to express great affection for something. The Greek term *sophos* is the word for "wisdom". If you know a woman whose name is Sophia, it means "wise woman." So philosophy can also be defined as the love of wisdom.

What is wisdom? Some people equate wisdom with knowledge and mistakenly think that intelligent people are also wise. However, most know that this is not true. I am sure we can all think of people who are smart but not wise. Wisdom has less to do with how much one knows and more to do with how one uses the knowledge one has. This does not mean that knowledge is unimportant. One sign of the truly wise person is that she will attempt to learn as much as she can. However, wisdom is more than having knowledge. Knowledge is necessary for wisdom, but it is not sufficient. Wisdom is knowledge applied. It is using the knowledge one has in a way that benefits one's life. This is the kind of wisdom personified in Proverbs 4:5-12:

Acquire wisdom! Acquire understanding!
Do not forget nor turn away from the words of my mouth.
"Do not forsake her, and she will guard you;
Love her, and she will watch over you.
"The beginning of wisdom is: Acquire wisdom;
And with all your acquiring, get understanding.
"Prize her, and she will exalt you;
She will honor you if you embrace her.
"She will place on your head a garland of grace;
She will present you with a crown of beauty."

Hear, my son, and accept my sayings
And the years of your life will be many.
I have directed you in the way of wisdom;
I have led you in upright paths.
When you walk, your steps will not be impeded;
And if you run, you will not stumble.

In the New Testament, Paul uses the description "spiritual man" in his letter to the Corinthians to describe the wise person: "He who is spiritual appraises all things" (1 Cor 2:15). To appraise something means to investigate it and determine its value. That is an excellent description of what philosophers do. They examine beliefs and determine their value. If you are a lover of wisdom, then philosophy is the field for you.

These definitions help, but something a little more tangible is necessary. Here is a suggested working definition of philosophy: *Philosophy is the critical examination of our foundational beliefs concerning the nature of reality, knowledge and truth, and our moral and social values.* This may not be a perfect definition; there are some who will quibble with it. But it is a good working definition. However, it requires explanation.

First, philosophy is the critical examination of beliefs. The term *critical* might communicate the wrong idea. The word is often used in a negative sense, as in, "You are so critical this morning. What happened? Did you get up on the wrong side of the bed?" This comment conveys that the person is displaying a bad attitude. However, that is not the way philosophers employ the term. They mean "critical" in the sense of "analytical"—a critical mind, not a critical heart. In this sense, a person is critical if, rather than accepting what he reads or hears, he takes time to analyze it. There are three main tasks in analyzing: clarification, justification and evaluation. To clarify something means to determine what it means. Justification addresses the questions: Is this true, and are there good reasons to believe that it is true? Evaluation determines the value or significance of the idea. The previous discussion of Socrates' claim, "The unexamined life is not worth living," is a good example of critical examination.

This discussion started with the question of clarification: What did he mean by "the unexamined life," and what did he mean by "not worth living"? Then it addressed the question of justification: Is it true that the unexamined life is not worth living? Finally, in the illustration of Wonmug, the discussion turned to evaluating the significance of living a life of seeking truth rather than a life of seeking happiness.

If philosophy involves critical examination, the next question is, What do philosophers examine? The definition says "foundational beliefs." A belief may be defined as an idea or concept one accepts or affirms as true.[12] People express beliefs in propositions: Abraham Lincoln was once president of the United States.[13] We all have many different beliefs about many different things, and they can be categorized a number of ways: true or false, important or trivial, likely or remote, dispositional or considered. While we are often conscious of some of our beliefs, we hold many beliefs that we may not be thinking about currently or that we assume and have never thought about. The belief about Lincoln is an example of a belief I am sure you hold and yet were not thinking about until this moment. Not all beliefs are foundational beliefs. For example, the belief about Abraham Lincoln is not a foundational belief. Foundational beliefs are those beliefs that are central and fundamental to an overall worldview and yet are often not thought about. Philosophers examine all kinds of beliefs, but they tend to concentrate on these central beliefs because they form the core and are the basis of all our other beliefs.

Another term we might use to describe these foundational beliefs is *presuppositions*. Presuppositions are beliefs people usually do not think about or try to prove. They are assumptions people hold about themselves and the world, without which they would not be able to arrive at any other knowledge. Because presuppositions affect all other beliefs, philosophers think it important to examine them critically to determine what they really mean, whether they are true and their significance.

What is the content of foundational beliefs? The above definition lists three major categories of foundational beliefs: beliefs about reality, beliefs about knowledge and truth, and beliefs about moral and social

---

[12]I am aware that a more nuanced definition of belief would draw out several other considerations, such as dispositional states and self-deception, but this straightforward definition will work for our purposes.

[13]New philosophy students sometimes confuse "belief" and "fact" and mistakenly think they are mutually exclusive. They think "belief" is a subjective opinion while a "fact" is an objective truth claim. This is a common confusion between ontology (what is real) and epistemology (what I know). A fact is an ontological entity, a particular state of affairs in reality. A belief is what one thinks about that state of affairs. It is true that when the evidence for a belief is strong, we often tend to call the belief a fact. But this is a misuse of the term. It is a well-established belief. Beliefs and facts are not mutually incompatible; they are two different categories. So the statement, "Abraham Lincoln was once president of the United States," expresses a belief about a fact.

values.[14] Individuals hold presuppositions in all three areas. Here are some examples.[15]

One part of reality is the existence of creatures called human beings. We hold a number of foundational beliefs about human beings. For example, most of us believe that human beings have free will. Free will is the idea that humans can deliberate about their actions and beliefs and make choices based on those deliberations. Because they are free and could have done otherwise, they are held responsible for those choices. Many people do not often think about free will; they assume it in their evaluations of the actions of others. It is a presupposition. However, a number of philosophers have wondered whether people really are free to make choices. There are many forces outside a person's control that have large bearing on what he decides. The environment he was raised in and the circumstances that happen to come about have a great deal to do with the character a person develops. Because actions often flow out of character, many philosophers wonder whether people are as free as they think they are. These philosophers might argue that there are many times when people do not have free will and therefore cannot be held responsible for their actions. Free will may not be as easy to affirm as we may have originally assumed.

Another basic belief can be found in the realm of knowledge and truth. People believe they know things, and much of this knowledge is based on their experiences. Such knowledge comes primarily in two modes: what we are currently experiencing (the sensations we are having right now) and past experiences in the form of memories. Let us examine these separately.

Most people assume that their memories are reliable. When they reflect on an event in the past, they believe they are remembering the event correctly, especially if it is recent. But can we really know if our memories are reliable? In order to be sure, it seems that we would need a way to test the reliability of memories. In medical laboratories, re-

[14]As we will see in chapter four, these three categories form the three major divisions of philosophy: metaphysics, epistemology and axiology.
[15]My purpose is merely to illustrate the different kinds of beliefs of which we have presuppositions. It is not my purpose to enter into a detailed discussion of these issues.

searchers practice an activity called quality control. These are a series of tests performed on diagnostic instruments to make sure they are providing accurate information. What kind of diagnostic test can we devise to assess whether or not our memories are reliable? Suppose Chris says, "I can think of a time when I parked my car outside my office, went inside for a while, came back out and remembered where I parked my car. My memory was reliable that time." However, this test is inadequate because it depends on a memory to test whether memories are reliable. Chris might respond, "I will just check out my memory of an event with someone else's memory of the same event, and if they correlate, then that means my memory is reliable." However, this is the same problem, because she is using a memory (someone else's this time) to test whether her memories are reliable. If there is no noncircular way to test whether memories are reliable, then how can we know that what they tell us is true? Doesn't knowledge require good (noncircular) evidence? How do we know our memories were not planted inside of us and do not correspond with reality at all?

"Certainly we can be sure of our immediate sensations," Chris might say. "I know what I am seeing right now." People assume that their current sense experience, what they are seeing, hearing and feeling right now, gives them knowledge about the world. We *see* a tree outside the window, so there must *be* a tree outside the window. In order to know that our senses are reliable, we again need a way to perform quality control on them. But how could we test the reliability of our senses? We cannot get outside of our sense experience to observe whether what our senses tell us is really the case. The problem is that it is possible for our senses to deceive us and that what we think we are experiencing is not really there. In the motion picture *The Matrix*, that was exactly the experience of Neo. Unknown to him, his brain was attached to a supercomputer that was controlling all of his sensations.[16] He thought he was experiencing certain events, but every sensation he

---

[16]This concept was first made popular by philosopher Hillary Putnam and is often called the brain-in-the-vat scenario. But the original idea goes back to René Descartes when he suggested the possibility of an evil demon controlling our sensations. A hit multimillion-dollar movie—who says philosophy is not practical?

had was a creation of the computer. If such a scenario is possible, can we be sure of anything we are currently experiencing? Perhaps the idea of knowledge based on personal experience is not as obvious as we might first think.

We also have assumptions when it comes to values. We believe that some things are better than other things and often rank them according to their value. We say, "This movie (book, song, idea) is better than that one." What is the basis for this ranking? Many people believe it is purely personal preference and individual taste. A common cliché that expresses this idea states: "Beauty is in the eye of the beholder." However, is this true? Is the ranking of values nothing more than *just* individual preferences? If that is the case, why are there art museums in which art critics recognize certain works of art as great (with the implied converse that some are not), or programs like the Academy Awards in which members of the academy try to recognize the best movies and performances of the year? In these contexts "great" and "best" imply that there is some objectively recognized standard for some works being better than others. Maybe there is more to beauty than just personal preferences. Most of us would be more than a little shocked if *Plan 9 from Outer Space* beat *Schindler's List* as best picture.[17] The assumption about beauty being in the eye of the beholder is open to debate.

These are all examples of common foundational beliefs people have about reality (we have free will), knowledge (knowledge based on personal experience is possible) and values (some things are better than others). Each of these beliefs is central to our worldview and affects many of our decisions and other beliefs. Yet even this brief discussion shows they are not as obvious as we might have originally assumed. This kind of analysis is the task of philosophy: the critical examination of foundational beliefs we hold about the nature of reality, knowledge and truth, and our moral and social values.

---

[17]If you have never seen *Plan 9 from Outer Space* (1959), you should rent it if you want to see an excruciatingly bad movie. In fact, it is so bad it is a fun film to watch, maybe more enjoyable than *Schindler's List*. But there is a difference between a movie being fun and its being good. *Plan 9* may be fun, but it is not good.

DESCRIBING PHILOSOPHY

A second way to get to know something is to describe it. Definitions are the skeleton of an idea, while descriptions put flesh on the skeleton. The above definition of philosophy provides a basic idea about what it is. Describing philosophy draws out the finer details and subtle nuances. When we describe something, we list its characteristics or properties. Although there are a number of distinguishing features to philosophy, there are six that will provide us with a more nuanced understanding of philosophy.[18]

1. The relationship between philosophy and facts. Many disciplines are concerned about discovering and knowing facts. Historians strive to find out the facts of what happened in the past. Scientists study to understand the facts of the world around us: what is happening, how it happens and why. Mathematicians attempt to understand the facts about mathematical truths and to use these in understanding facts about the world. However, philosophy is different in how it relates to facts. Philosophers are generally more interested in what lies behind the facts, their meaning, significance and veracity, than in the facts themselves.

Suppose your friend Bill tells you he is in the market for a new car and wants to buy the best car he can afford. If we were to ask what the facts are in this case, the answer is straightforward: Bill wants to buy the best car available. But if we were to probe more deeply, we might ask what Bill means by "best" car. There are many different criteria we can use for "best" in this case. Perhaps he means the newest car. Perhaps he means the oldest car (an antique). Perhaps he means the fastest car or the best-looking car. Maybe he is thinking of the one with the nicest interior features. The point is that while we know what Bill said, the meaning behind what he said needs clarification. Even after we clarify what he meant by "best" there is still the question of significance and truthfulness. Assuming by "best" he means the nicest-looking car, we can still question whether this is the correct criterion to use or which car satisfies the description. When we try to get behind the facts to determine

---

[18]I am indebted to my studies with Dr. Norman L. Geisler for much of the original germ of these six characteristics.

their meaning, truthfulness or significance, we are doing philosophy.

Here is another example. The Mormon religion claims that its founder, Joseph Smith Jr., had a religious experience in which an angel named Moroni claiming to be from God appeared before him and told him if he excavated a certain site on a hill called Cumorah in upstate New York, he would find several golden plates with writing on them. When translated, they would tell the story of Jesus' postresurrection appearances to a group of native Americans called the Nephites. Joseph Smith claims to have followed the angel's directions, and that is where the Book of Mormon, the foundational scriptures of the Mormon religion, came from. Assuming these events occurred as reported by Smith, does that automatically authenticate Mormonism as divinely ordained?

Not necessarily. Even if these events took place as described, it does not explain their meaning or significance.[19] No experience comes with its own interpretation built in. Experiences have to be interpreted and analyzed according to some criteria to determine their meaning. There are a variety of possible explanations of Smith's experience. For example, Scripture tells us that Satan can appear as an angel of light (2 Cor 11:14) with the purpose of deceiving and leading others astray. If Scripture is used as the criterion, then there are a number of discrepancies between the Book of Mormon and Scripture that would call the divine origin of the Book of Mormon into question. How do we determine the criteria? That, too, is a philosophical issue. The point here is that philosophy is concerned with more than just the facts. Factual data alone rarely solve philosophical problems or settle hard questions.

2. _The importance of method in philosophical investigation._ It often surprises people to learn that philosophy is not nearly as interested in what they believe as in why they believe it. The method an individual employs to arrive at a belief is extremely important to philosophers. In order to understand this, it is necessary to make an important distinction between first-order and second-order disciplines.

A first-order discipline is a field that studies reality directly. Biology is a good example of a first-order discipline. Biology is the study of dif-

---

[19]It should be noted that the facts of Joseph Smith's experience are in dispute. For the purposes of my illustration, we can assume the facts as described by Smith are true.

ferent kinds of life. It is done by directly observing different life forms and arriving at conclusions about them. For example, suppose a biologist wants to know whether frogs have lungs. How would she answer this question? By observation. She dissects a frog, notes that it has lungs and concludes that frogs have lungs. In other words, direct observation of reality is the normal means by which biology and most sciences operate.

A second-order discipline is a field that studies the methods and presuppositions of first-order disciplines. It is not interested in the conclusion as much as the means used to arrive at the conclusion and the presuppositions held while attempting to answer the question. In the previous example, the biologist wanted to know whether frogs have lungs, and she answered the question by dissecting a frog and observing its lungs. However, did she answer the question asked? The question asked was, Do frogs have lungs? The biologist looked at only one frog. The question was not about this frog but about frogs as a species. Can a biologist arrive at a conclusion about an entire species by looking at only one representative? Not really. So the method used by our biologist is questionable and leaves the original question unanswered. How many frogs does she have to observe before our biologist can know whether frogs have lungs? That is a philosophical debate about the method used in arriving at truth.

Another issue involved in the biologist's answer has to do with some of her presuppositions that are fundamentally philosophical. In answering the question the way she did, she was assuming a particular position on the metaphysical question of universals (Do all frogs share a universal property called "frogness"?). She also assumed that a principle called the uniformity of nature was in force. This is the idea that there is a uniformity of characteristics common among the members of species. All frogs have the same basic characteristics, like lungs. Critically examining such presuppositions is one of the tasks of philosophy.

3. One of the primary tasks of philosophy is clarification. According to the given definition, one aspect of critical examination is clarification. The important role clarification plays in doing philosophy cannot be emphasized enough. Philosophy is interested in finding the truth, and clear thinking is a key ingredient in that search. There are two great enemies to clear thinking: ambiguity and vagueness. A term is ambiguous when there is more than one possible meaning. An example is the term *right*. Think of all the different ways this term can be used. It can be used of a direction, as in "right or left"; it can be used in a morally normative sense, as in "it is right to tell the truth"; it can be used in a rationally normative sense, as in "that was the right answer to the problem"; and it can be used in the sense of a legal claim we can make, as in "I have a right to an attorney." With all these possible meanings, it is understandable when people confuse these different uses. A friend once commented to me, "A woman has a legal right to an abortion; therefore it is right for her to get one." He was confusing the morally normative use with the legal-claim use of the term.

A term is vague when the meaning is not clear.[20] Vagueness has to do with the inability to identify the parameters of a term. For example, take the word *heap*, as in, "That's a heap of food on your plate." What exactly is a heap? It is obviously more than a couple of items, but how much more? The point where something crosses the line from not being a heap to being a heap is unclear. Vagueness often occurs when a term is overused. The term is used so often and in so many different contexts that its meaning, if it ever had one, gets lost. This can be easily demonstrated by noting one of the vaguest terms in the English language: *love*. What does one mean when one uses this term? Like *heap*, its meaning is not always clear.

Christians are often guilty of vague thinking. They use Christian terms and clichés without knowing exactly what they mean. They often merely mimic or affirm what everybody else says. Here is a humorous example. Most Christians have probably gone through the experience of sitting down for a meal where someone opens with a prayer in which he

[20]The literature among professional philosophers on vagueness is impressive and goes well beyond what suffices for present purposes. In general, though, vagueness comes from our inability to identify the clear criteria for the application of a term. Imagine an object that loses its atoms one at a time. Eventually the object—suppose it is a chair—will cease being a chair, but when? With the removal of what atom does the chair cease to exist? It is notoriously hard to say. Efforts of philosophers to address the ubiquitous challenge of vagueness in language have run the gamut from fuzzy logic to supervaluationism to epistemicism. Such complexities need not detain us here, where a more colloquial and rough-and-ready account of vagueness will do. The vagueness of most concern for our discussion is the result of the needlessly sloppy overuse of certain words.

says, "Lord, bless this food to the nourishment of our bodies." This is a good and common thing to pray at the beginning of a meal. But Christians need to stop and consider what it is they are asking God to do. They are asking him to "bless the food." But what does it mean to "bless" something? This is a term used frequently in Christian circles, and yet rarely does anyone know what it means. The original derivation of the Hebrew term means "to make better or to make happy."[21] Are people asking God to make the food taste better or happy? Maybe this is the origin of the McDonald's Happy Meal. In what sense could God make the food better? Perhaps the answer is found in the other part of the prayer, where the person asks God to make the food "nourishing to our bodies." But didn't God already do this when he created the food and created our bodies with the means to convert it into nourishment? Is there now some additional act God needs to do to make it nourishing? Is unblessed food less nourishing?

I am being a bit jocular here, and I am not saying there is anything wrong with saying this prayer before meals. But people often use language in an ambiguous or vague manner without thinking about what they are saying or believing. Philosophers hold that foundational beliefs are too important to be needlessly vague or ambiguous. Hence, as a discipline, they take clarification seriously. This is why philosophers will often begin a philosophical discussion by taking the time to define terminology and concepts. They want to make sure everyone is on the same page. When we engage in philosophical discussions in my classes, I will often ask a student, "What do you mean when you use that term or phrase?" This can be frustrating to students new to philosophy. It seems as if philosophers are being too analytical and overly detailed when they do this. They are not. They believe that language should be employed carefully in the discussion of philosophical issues.[22]

4. *Philosophy examines and evaluates everything. Nothing is taken for granted.* In philosophy, every belief and idea is open to critical ex-

---

[21] The term in Hebrew, *barak*, has about as many usages as its English equivalent "bless." It is also translated "to kneel," often times when offering a gift. In most settings in which it is used of God it means to make things better or happier for someone.

[22] It is often said that it is possible to do too much analyzing. I do not deny this. However, in my experience it is not a danger most students need to worry about.

amination. Philosophers require clarification and justification before accepting any belief as true. Even the nature and definition of philosophy itself is discussed and debated by philosophers. In this sense, as a field, philosophy trumps all other fields. It is not coincidental that the highest academic degree in most fields is doctor of philosophy in _____. For no matter which field an individual studies, whether it is science, history, literature or the arts, each field ultimately comes down to foundational beliefs of what it is, why it works the way it does and how it works. Those are philosophical questions and require philosophical answers.

J. P. Moreland tells the story of having a discussion with a scientist. The scientist asked him what he did for a living, and he replied that he taught philosophy. The scientist rolled his eyes and scoffed, "Philosophy! I used to be interested in those things when I was a teenager, but I outgrew it. I now know that the only knowledge of reality is that which can be quantified and tested in the laboratory. If you can measure it and test it scientifically you can know it. If not, the topic is nothing but private opinion and idle speculation."[23] Moreland looked at him and said, "Really? Can you give me a scientific definition of 'science'? Can you scientifically demonstrate that science is the only discipline that is objectively rational and true? Or provide a scientific explanation for the value of scientific explanations?" What Moreland was trying to point out is that the very nature and presuppositions of science, its aims, methodologies and values, cannot be validated by science because they are ultimately philosophical questions, not scientific ones. When a scientist addresses these questions, he is no longer functioning in the role of a scientist but is functioning as a philosopher. Philosophy cannot be avoided, nor can it be responsibly ignored or trivialized. The question is not whether people will end up doing philosophy or not, but how well they will do it when they must.

Some Christians are apprehensive about the idea that philosophy examines and evaluates everything. They often say, "Does that include God and the Bible? Aren't you placing human fallen reason above God?

---

[23]This view, sometimes called scientism, says that the only knowledge claims that can be true are those that can be scientifically verified.

What about faith? The Scriptures say we should have the faith of a child. We're not supposed to question God. God said it, I believe it, and that settles it." These Christians are sincere and right-hearted, but they also are wrong-headed about the place of reason in relation to faith for a number of reasons.[24]

First, although it is true that God has ontological priority, reason has epistemological priority. To say that God has ontological priority means that God is first and ultimate in the order of being or existence. God exists above everything, and all things find their origin, value and meaning in him. Also, by giving God ontological priority we recognize that he is the source for our ability to reason and understand. Reason is a gift from God to humans to assist them in understanding God and the world God has made. A number of Christian philosophers have recently made the case that cognition, the ability to reason and know, is not possible in a world without God.[25]

However, in the order of knowing, reason comes first. Theologian and philosopher Norman Geisler affirms this point when he writes:

While God is prior to logic in the order of being (ontologically) nevertheless, logic is prior to God in the order of knowing (epistemologically). No knowledge is possible without the laws of thought; if this is not true then nothing else follows. Even the statement "God is God" makes no sense if the law of identity does not hold.[26]

Geisler is speaking specifically of logic, but I am using "reason" in a more broad sense as referring to all of the cognitive faculties involved in gaining knowledge, including but not limited to logical abilities, learning, reflecting, deliberating, remembering, understanding, and our moral faculties. Reason, in this broad sense, is the essential cognitive process individuals employ to know anything at all. Nothing can be known

[24]We cannot dwell on all the problems with these objections. The reader is recommended to read J. P. Moreland, *Love Your God with All Your Mind* (Colorado Springs: NavPress, 1997) for a fuller treatment.

[25]See Alvin Plantinga, *Where the Conflict Really Lies* (New York: Oxford University Press, 2011), pp. 31-350; Victor Reppert, *C. S. Lewis's Dangerous Idea* (Downers Grove, IL: InterVarsity Press, 2003), pp. 72-85; C. S. Lewis, *Miracles: A Preliminary Study* (New York: Macmillan, 1987), pp. 12-24; and J. P. Moreland, *The Recalcitrant Imago Dei: Human Persons and the Failure of Naturalism* (London: SCM Press, 2009), pp. 67-103.

[26]Norman L. Geisler, *Systematic Theology*, vol. 1 (Minneapolis: Bethany House, 2002), p. 90.

about God apart from our cognitive abilities because no knowledge of any kind can be obtained apart from them. We cannot even understand what the Bible says without our basic reasoning abilities. Every time a person opens the pages of Scripture and attempts to understand what is written there, she is interpreting, and interpretation is a philosophical activity. She is reasoning about the meaning, significance and application of Scripture based on a set of accepted criteria. Most people may never have thought about these criteria—it is one of the presuppositions they have when they approach Scripture. However, these interpretive criteria are philosophical principles that have been carefully reasoned and established by the community of believers down through the ages. [27]

None of this is to deny the important role of the Holy Spirit in aiding us to understand the things of God. I am not claiming that reason acts alone in this regard. The Christian church has always taught that the Holy Spirit plays a primary role in illuminating us concerning the understanding and application of Scripture. Reason does not displace the role of the Spirit. There is no dichotomy between reason and the Holy Spirit. They work together; the Holy Spirit uses our cognitive abilities in fulfilling this task. It is like using a hammer to drive a nail into a board. If we were to ask what caused the nail to go into the board, some might say the hammer while others may say the person wielding the hammer. In fact it is both. The person is the efficient cause, the power that causes the nail to go into the board, while the hammer is the instrumental cause, the tool employed, to cause the nail to go into the board. In the same way, reason is one of the primary instruments the Holy Spirit employs in illuminating, interpreting and applying God's Word in our lives.

Second, many Christians have adopted an unbiblical concept of faith as blind faith. Faith is important, but Scripture never promotes the idea of blind faith—believing anything with no reasons at all. That is not biblical faith; it is foolhardy presumption. Biblical faith believes God for what he has said he will do. This is not blind faith, for God has demonstrated over and over that he is trustworthy. J. P. Moreland and William Lane Craig write:

[27]See chapter three for more on the value of reason for the Christian, as well its importance in interpretation.

The biblical notion of faith involves three components: *notitia* (understanding the content of the Christian faith), *fiducia* (trust), and *assensus* (the assent of the intellect to the truth of some proposition). Trust is based on understanding, knowledge and the intellect's assent to truth. Belief *in* rests on belief *that*. One is called to trust in what he or she has reason to give intellectual assent (*assensus*) to. In Scripture, faith involves placing trust in what you have reason to believe is true. Faith is not a blind, irrational leap in the dark.[28]

Abraham is the perfect example of a person of faith. It is sometimes claimed that Abraham exhibited blind faith when he willingly obeyed God's command to sacrifice his son Isaac. However, Abraham apparently knew that Isaac would survive the sacrifice. Note the command to his servants when they arrived at the base of the mountain: "Stay here with the donkey, and I and the lad will go over there; and *we* will worship and return to you" (Gen 22:5, emphasis added). The author of Hebrews explains that in this incident Abraham "considered that God is able to raise people even from the dead" (Heb 11:19). Was this blind faith on Abraham's part? No, because God had proved himself trustworthy to Abraham several times. God promised him a land and came through. He promised Abraham a son when Sarah was beyond childbearing years and fulfilled that promise. Most important, he told Abraham that the descendants of his son Isaac would be as numerable as the stars of heaven. Because Isaac had no children at the time of his sacrifice, Abraham trusted that God was either not going to kill him or would raise him from the dead. That is not blind faith.

When John the Baptist was imprisoned and expressed doubts about who Jesus was, he sent his disciples to ask Jesus, "Are you the Expected One, or do we look for someone else?" (Lk 7:19). What was the response of Jesus? It was not, "Well, John, you just need to have more faith." No, what he said was, "Go and report to John what you have seen and heard: the blind receive sight, the lame walk, the lepers are cleansed, and the deaf hear, the dead are raised up, the poor have the gospel preached to them" (Lk 7:22). Jesus gave John reasons to believe that he was the

[28]J. P. Moreland and William Lane Craig, *Philosophical Foundations for a Christian Worldview* (Downers Grove, IL: InterVarsity Press, 2003), p. 18, emphasis in the original.

promised Messiah. Jesus did not ask his disciples to believe blindly, but he provided "many convincing proofs" (Acts 1:3) of his claims. He even made the same offer to his opponents: "If I do not do the works of My Father, do not believe me; but if I do them, though you do not believe Me, believe the works, so that you may know and understand that the Father is in Me, and I in the Father" (Jn 10:37-38).

In the same way we are not called to believe blindly. It is true that, unlike Abraham and John the Baptist, many of us have not had a direct personal experience of God.[29] But that does not mean that our faith is groundless. We do have reasons to believe based on the authority of the testimony of those who have had those experiences: the prophets and the apostles. If challenged as to why we should believe this testimony, we can offer reasons to hold that this testimony is reliable and true.[30] Whatever reasons we offer, whether it be a philosophical argument for God's existence, an argument for scriptural reliability or a personal encounter with God in the form of an answered prayer, miraculous healing or the convicting work of the Holy Spirit, we are not expected or required to abandon reason and take a blind leap of faith in believing that the claims of Christianity are true. We all choose to believe for some reason. If not, then why select Christianity over some other religion or nonreligion? There is no dichotomy between faith and reason. They work together. That is why Peter writes that we all should be able to "give an account for the hope that is within you" (1 Pet 3:15).

More could be said here, but the important point to remember is that the truth can stand up to scrutiny and examination. If the claims of Christians are true, then we have nothing to worry about from critical examination. In fact, such examination will enhance our faith as we clarify what we believe and establish good reasons to believe it.

5. Philosophy is usually concerned with foundational issues that have been perennial throughout the history of humankind. I am some-

---

[29]This is not to deny that many people claim to have genuine religious experiences where God is present to them in a real way. Many Christians will testify to answered prayer as God working in their lives. Others have experienced miraculous healings. There are also those who suggest that we have within us a *sensus divinitatis*, an inward sense of the divine that, under proper conditions, would enlighten us to God.

[30]This is the task of Christian apologetics. See chapter three for a fuller explanation.

times asked, "Why did you go into philosophy as a career?" My answer is always the same: I want to spend my life dealing with the important questions in life, the ones that really matter. That is what philosophy is about. It deals with humankind's most important issues. These issues have been around ever since humankind has been on earth: Are people free or determined? Is the human being just a physical body, or is there an immaterial aspect as well? What is the good, and how does one know when it is achieved? Is there such a thing as truth? Is there a God, and how does one know that and relate to him?

In medicine, there are not enough resources to be able to help all those who need help. For example, only a limited number of organs are available for transplantation to those who need them. Who gets access to the few organs we have, and who does not? This raises a question of justice. What is the just way to distribute scarce goods in a society? The question of justice is also the primary question in Plato's greatest work, *The Republic*. Although he was not dealing with the question of medical transplants, he was dealing with the same ultimate question of what a just society is and how goods and services should be distributed in such a society. Humankind has been dealing with the same questions since the beginning of recorded time.

Because these issues have been discussed for millennia, most philosophers realize they are probably not going to solve them today. This causes some people to be skeptical about philosophy. They reason, "If we have been trying to answer the same questions for thousands of years, and we haven't found answers by now, then what's the use? Maybe there are no answers, and we can't know anything about these ultimate questions."

The problem is not that there are no answers; the problem is that there are too many. Throughout the history of philosophy, many philosophers have offered competing theories as attempts to answer these ultimate questions. Although this might create even more skepticism on the part of some, there are two points to consider. First, there is value in taking the time to reflect critically on these fundamental issues. The process of deep reflection itself is affirming to our humanity. Second, not all proposed solutions are of the same quality. Some feature better arguments than others. The task of the philosopher is to sift through all the possible proposed solutions and arrive at the one that provides the best evidence or explanation.

This raises another important aspect of philosophy. Philosophers can often look at the same evidence and generate completely different explanations and theories to account for it. This is one of the most difficult aspects of philosophy for new students to grasp. Just because two philosophers disagree does not mean that one is rational and the other is not. It is possible to be rational and still be wrong. It is not always clear why this is the case, but there is a difference between a philosophical theory being rational, in the sense that the conclusion follows from the evidence, and it being compelling. For a view to be rational generally means that it is supported by the evidence or arguments in accordance with our perceptual abilities, memories, laws and rules of logic and our basic moral intuitions. To be compelling often involves many other factors such as our starting point, the set of beliefs we already hold, and a host of other psychological factors. It is possible for a point of view to be rational to one person and still not be compelling enough to motivate another to agree with it. For example, one might be able to explain how it is logically possible for a loving God to exist and yet there still be suffering and evil in the world. Such arguments might not be compelling to the individual who is currently going through the emotional turmoil of the loss of a child. Some persons have different evidential sets based on their experiences where they do not find any argument, not matter how rational, to be compelling.

This is another characteristic of philosophy. Philosophers are accustomed to disagreeing with one another, and they have come to accept that as a part of philosophy. They continue to present arguments in hopes of swaying others to see things from their point of view. But it does not bother most philosophers that there is disagreement. They usually respect one another even though they think the other is wrong. That is part of the nature and beauty of philosophy. Philosophers are free to explore and respectfully discuss new ideas with colleagues without the worry of personally offending them. It is even possible to be close friends with philosophers with whom one strongly disagrees.

6. Philosophy often appeals to systems of principles or guidelines *regarded to be true.* Philosophy is not done in a vacuum, and philosophical examination does not begin from a neutral position. The idea of the completely neutral philosopher is a myth. Everyone has presuppositions and even biases that guide their thinking about foundational beliefs. The idea is not to ignore or abandon such presuppositions so much as to be aware of them and their effect on one's thinking, and be willing to change them if necessary. Those least aware of their own biases are most likely to be held in bondage to them.

Philosophers build systems of beliefs. In order to do that, they begin with guidelines or first principles that they hold to be true and then, using these, investigate new knowledge claims as they arise. If those claims are inconsistent with what they already consider true, an adjustment must be made. Inconsistency with a set of beliefs is a sign of falsehood. This usually means philosophers must do one of two things: either reject the new claim as true or adjust their system to adapt to this new claim.

For example, one system of guidelines most philosophers employ in critical examination is the classical laws of logic. The foundation for logic is the principle of noncontradiction, which states that something cannot both be and not be at the same time and in the same sense. If a new claim presents a contradiction to an accepted belief, then that is a sign that something is wrong, and either the new claim or the prior belief needs to be rejected. They cannot both be true according to this law of logic.[31]

Another example of a system of beliefs is science. Some of the basic laws in science are the laws of physics. These laws help us to comprehend the universe and guide us in performing tasks. When NASA sent men to the moon in the 1960s, it employed the basic laws of physics to guide them in planning out each step along the way: the amount of thrust necessary to escape Earth's gravitational pull, when and where midcourse corrections were needed, the amount of fuel necessary to land on the moon, the exact angle necessary for the spacecraft to reenter Earth's atmosphere.

[31]Some may ask, "But how do we know the law of noncontradiction is a reliable guide?" Chapter five will address this question.

It is true that sometimes the system itself needs to be examined. A new claim can be so forceful it causes a reevaluation of the system. In general, the more established a system is, the more rarely this will happen. But it does happen on occasion. When it does, the system needs to be adapted to accommodate the new claim. For example, Christians hold to the reality of miracles, which many think violate the laws of physics. However, one way of thinking of a miracle is not as a violation of the laws of physics but as the interference of a supernatural agent on the laws. By analogy, persons often interfere with the laws of physics. If a person accidentally drops an object, the law of gravity takes over and the object falls to the ground. However, if the person catches the object before it hits the ground, then he or she has interfered with the law of gravity. Miracles can be seen as the actions of a supernatural agent who has the power to interfere with the laws of physics. Assuming the evidence for a miracle is strong, this is a case in which science needs either to adapt the system to allow for the new claim or rule out the possibility of a supernatural agent.

Pulling these different systems of beliefs together constitutes a worldview. The next chapter will address the importance of a worldview, but for now the definition of a worldview is this: a comprehensive system of beliefs that functions, first, as an explanation and interpretation of the world and, second, as an application of that system to the way people live and the values they hold. Philosophy builds worldviews.

Contrasting and Comparing Philosophy with Other Disciplines

Along with defining and describing philosophy, a third way to get to know what it is involves comparing and contrasting it with other fields. To compare two things is to note their similarities, and to contrast them is to note their differences. People often use this method as a way to understand or explain something new. When they read a new book or see a new movie, they will often appeal to similar books or movies as a way to describe it to others: "It's just like *Star Wars* but funnier." This section examines three fields that are similar in many ways to philosophy but are also different enough to elucidate telling distinctions between them and philosophy.

Philosophy and religion. It is not always easy to draw a line between philosophy and religion. Some religions are very philosophical, especially Eastern religions such as Hinduism and Buddhism. But there are some general comments we can make. Philosophy and religion are similar in that they both search for the ultimate—that which has ultimate meaning and value, the one thing that unifies everything and from which everything finds its meaning and origin. Most religions refer to the ultimate in divine terms: God, Yahweh, Allah or Brahmin. Some of these religions believe God is a person, and some do not. But almost all religions believe that he or it is where the ultimate lies. Although some philosophers have given up the search for anything ultimate beyond our material world, much of the history of philosophy chronicles the quest for that which unifies all things. Philosophers often refer to the object of their search simply as the "ultimate."

Where philosophy and religion often differ is in how they conduct that search. Religion usually appeals to some authoritative revelation to discover the truths about the ultimate. For Christians, it is the Bible. For Jewish believers, it is Torah and the Talmud. For Muslims, it is the Qur'an. Eastern religions appeal to a much broader range of writings. Most Buddhists appeal to the writings of Buddha as found in the *Pali Tipitaka* and the *Mahayana Sutras* as authoritative. Hindus appeal to two groups of writings: the collection of Vedas found in the *Shruti*, and a collection of epic poems referred to as the *Smriti*, the most well-known being the *Bhagavad Gita*. Different religions and different branches within religions place different values on these writings, but authoritative religious scriptures are usually an important part in understanding the ultimate.

In contrast, philosophy uses rational inquiry in attempting to understand the ultimate. Although there are many great philosophical books and treatises, none has assumed authority over the others. Generally, philosophers are suspicious of any book claiming to be authoritative. Christians may believe that the Scriptures are the inspired Word of God and may even have good reasons for believing so, but many philosophers will withhold judgment on such a claim, leaving it to each rational thinker to decide.[32] For philosophy, the search for the ultimate is an exercise in critical reflection, not something one accepts because some authority claims it.

A brief comment on the relation between philosophy and theology is beneficial at this juncture. Broadly speaking, theology is the study of God. More narrowly, Christian theology critically examines the beliefs of the Christian community concerning the person and work of God. The source for information about God is his revelation of himself, which Christians generally divide into two types: general and special revelation. Scripture commends the significance of general revelation (Ps 19; Rom 1–2), but the primary and authoritative source for information about God comes from special revelation, especially the Scriptures of the Old and New Testaments. The task of the theologian is to take the raw data as they are presented in Scripture and derive coherent theological concepts, principles and doctrines. Philosophical reasoning is one of the tools employed by theologians as they perform this task. A famous aphorism states, "Theology is the queen of the sciences, and philosophy is her handmaiden." As we will see in chapter three, philosophy aids the theologian's task in a number of ways.

Another difference between philosophy and religion involves a spiritual aspect not normally found in philosophy. Religion usually incorporates spiritual disciplines such as prayer, meditation and worship, often expressed through liturgical rites and ceremonies. One does not find this spiritual dimension in philosophy. Therefore, while religion may have many characteristics in common with philosophy, it would be inappropriate to claim religion reduces to philosophy or vice versa.

Philosophy and science. Philosophy and science are similar in that both try to understand reality in a methodical fashion. They both use observation and appeal to evidence to support their conclusions. They both derive criteria, hypotheses and theories that they apply to specific situations to discover truth about reality. Because of this similarity, some have tried to reduce philosophy to a science.

However, there are a couple of important distinctions that reveal the

[32]Many philosophers also affirm that the Bible is the Word of God. We will discuss the role of the Bible in doing philosophy in chapter three.

disciplines are not the same and that one is not reducible to the other. The first has to do with the extent of their search. Science generally examines that part of reality experienced with the senses, what we might call the physical world. Most of the empirical sciences, such as biology, physics and chemistry, deal with the relations between physical substances or elements. In fact, some scientists believe that all that exists is the physical reality of matter and energy, a belief called scientific naturalism. Many of these scientists also adopt a corollary epistemological view we mentioned earlier, scientism—the notion that scientific knowledge is the only kind of knowledge there is.

Although philosophy also has some things to say about the physical world, its field extends outside physical reality to what lies beyond and behind it. Philosophy asks, Why is reality the way it is? Why are there these laws of physics instead of other laws? Where did reality come from? Is it one thing or many unrelated things? Is there a meaning and purpose behind reality, or is it meaningless and without value?

A second distinction between philosophy and science is that science deals with first-order questions about reality, while philosophy deals with second-order questions about disciplines like science. This is part of the problem with scientism. The very claim that scientific knowledge is the only kind of knowledge is self-refuting because the statement itself is not a first-order scientific claim; it is a second-order philosophical claim about the nature and limits of knowledge. Philosophy deals with several second-order questions about the presuppositions and nature of science: What are its parameters and limits? What methods does it use to discover knowledge, and how does one demonstrate that these methods are reliable? Are scientific theories actual descriptions of reality or just explanations that function as a means to solve problems? Why does the universe operate according to these laws of physics, and how did this operation begin? What are the sufficient and necessary conditions for something to be scientific knowledge? These distinctions show that that science and philosophy are not reducible to each other, yet they remain capable of fruitful dialogue.

Philosophy and art. Artists often use their medium to express philosophical ideas. This is one way that philosophy and art are similar. They often deal with similar topics as well. One of Vincent Van Gogh's last paintings was titled *The Wheat Field with Crows*. The painting depicts a wheat field on a beautiful summer day in 1890. The wheat is golden yellow, blowing in the wind and just ripe for harvest. The sky is bright blue with a few white clouds. Three paths of green grass cut through the middle and two sides of the field trailing off to the horizon. If the description were to end here, one might be left with the impression that Van Gogh was painting a beautiful landscape. However, above all of this he paints thick black clouds obscuring a large section of sky. Flying throughout the wheat field are black crows devouring the wheat. Shortly after completing this painting, Van Gogh committed suicide. Experts explain, from what they can tell from his letters, that he had arrived at the belief that life is ultimately meaningless and absurd. People are born and grow in a beautiful world. But always hovering above and in the background are the pains and sufferings of life. Ultimately, people die, and that is all there is to human existence. Life is no more meaningful and has no more value than the wheat that is eaten by the crows. Philosophers have a name for this depressing view of life: nihilism. Van Gogh was capturing artistically what some modern philosophers promote. That is where art and philosophy overlap.

However, this example also shows how art and philosophy differ. In general, art usually only conveys a particular philosophical view, whereas philosophy seeks the rational justification of a view. Philosophy argues for a view; art expresses it.[33] The Van Gogh painting does not give us reasons why we should accept that nihilism is a valid view of life. At most, the artist is expressing that it is the view of life that he has accepted. It is not in the nature of art *qua* art to provide arguments.

This is not to deny that there is a certain beauty to a well-structured argument. As a philosopher, I have read or heard a number of argu-

[33]This generalization about art is especially true of representational art (painting, sculpture) and some performing arts (dance, music). There are forms of artistic work where language is the medium of expression (literature, poetry, drama). In some of these cases an author, playwright or poet may produce an argument within the work as well as express a view.

ments. Some of them are impressive on the aesthetic level. I recently read an account by Christian philosopher Tom Morris relating the effect that C. S. Lewis had on him while Morris was a high school student:

I first read Lewis when I was in high school, and was completely mesmerized by his writing. His ability to cut through to the core of any issue, shine light on the most central elements of Christian belief and display Christian theology's penetrating grasp of human nature were, in my admittedly limited experience, unparalleled. Moreover, in deftly managing the daunting balance between a keen and easy accessibility of language together with a real logical rigor of thought conveyed by that language, he presented to many of his readers an immensely attractive example of what a public philosopher could be and do. As a college student, I recall finding in his books sentences of such insight, and unexpected phrases of such perfection, that I would just sit and stare at the words, thinking to myself, *I wish I had been able to say it that way. It was all so wise, and yet at the same time so simple. I was just astonished.*[34]

However, while philosophy can be expressed in an aesthetically pleasing manner, philosophy is distinct in that art is concerned mostly with structure, whereas philosophy is concerned mostly with content. One cannot be reduced to the other.[35]

The main point in this section is that, while philosophy has similarities with religion, science and art, it is its own distinct field of inquiry.

EXPERIENCING PHILOSOPHY

Philosophers often divide knowledge into two main types: propositional knowledge and experiential knowledge.[36] Propositional knowledge, as the name implies, consists of beliefs that can be formulated and conveyed in propositions. Much knowledge comes in this form, whether it be objective, as in history (the attack on the Alamo was in 1836), science (a carbon atom has six electrons) or math (1246/74 = 16.837), or whether

---

[34]Tom Morris, "Foreword," in *C. S. Lewis as Philosopher: Truth, Goodness and Beauty*, ed. David J. Baggett, Gary R. Habermas and Jerry L. Walls (Downers Grove, IL: InterVarsity Press, 2008), p. 9.
[35]The branch of philosophy devoted to the philosophy of art is called aesthetics. I discuss this more fully in chapter four.
[36]Experiential knowledge is often further divided into knowledge by acquaintance and competence or how-to knowledge.

it be subjective (I am hopeful that the Dodgers will win the National League pennant this year). Experiential knowledge is knowledge gained through experiencing something. It cannot be conveyed through propositions. Dave can talk about his experience—"I had a great time at the concert last night"—but cannot convey the experience itself in a proposition. No matter how many details Dave shares with Tom about his experience at the concert, Tom cannot know what it was like experientially unless Tom experiences it himself.[37]

It should be noted that neither of these forms of knowledge is superior to the other. They are different forms. However, it is also true that experiential knowledge often enhances our understanding beyond what propositional knowledge can convey. A doctor does not have to experience a broken arm in order to understand what it is and how to treat it. However, if she has had a similar debilitation in her own experience, it is valuable in understanding the pain and disruption the broken arm causes her patient and can be helpful in her overall treatment of the patient.

This discussion of philosophy so far has been functioning on the propositional level. We have defined philosophy, described it and contrasted and compared it with similar fields. Propositionally, you, the reader, should have a fairly good idea of what philosophy is at this point. However, in order to know it for what it really is, you have to experience it. You might remember that philosophy can be used as a noun or as a verb. Philosophy is more than content and beliefs. It is a skill. Like any skill, the only way you can learn it is by doing it. And the more you do it, the better you will get.

Suppose you decide to learn to play the trumpet. A music teacher could lecture you on all the aspects involved in playing the trumpet. He could explain how to hold it, which valves to press in order to play specific notes, the correct embouchure to use while blowing into it and how to get just the right tone and vibrato while playing. He could also lecture you about reading and playing music: what the lines and spaces mean, how to read a key signature and the meter, the difference between a half

---

[37]And even then Tom still cannot know Dave's experience. He can know only his own. The fact that persons have inner subjective experiences that are not objectively reducible is one of the strongest arguments for an immaterial mind separate from the physical brain.

note and an eighth note. He can convey all these concepts propositionally. Would you then be able to play the trumpet? It is doubtful. It is not until you go into the practice room and work with the trumpet that you begin to learn to play it. That is the way you learn a skill—by doing it. Philosophy is like learning to play the trumpet. You cannot know it only by reading about it. You have to do it.

This book is an introduction to philosophy. It will give you a starting place, an overview of the terrain so you have an idea of what it is about. Other books provide a more detailed map of specific areas in philosophy to help you even more. These maps are valuable because they are written by those who have traveled through this terrain before you and can provide some guideposts while showing you interesting vistas and nasty pitfalls. However, you need to take the journey yourself. You have already begun doing that to a certain degree, for all people think about foundational beliefs at some time in their lives. Philosophy provides a formal means of structuring and reflecting on these experiences. The next two chapters will discuss why this journey is important.

two

WHY IS PHILOSOPHY IMPORTANT?

In *Gorgias*, Plato records a famous debate between Socrates and an older gentleman named Callicles. They are debating Socrates's claim that it is always better to suffer a wrong than to do it. At one point in the debate Callicles rails against the study of philosophy: "It is a pretty thing if you engage in it moderately in your youth; but if you continue in it longer than you should, it is the ruin of any man."[1] Callicles is convinced that the main objective of life is to obtain wealth and honor, neither of which the study of philosophy achieves. "It is a good thing to engage in philosophy just so far as it is an aid to education . . . [but] when I see an older man still studying philosophy and not deserting it, that man, Socrates, is actually asking for a whipping."[2] Is Callicles right? Is the study of philosophy a waste of time? Does philosophical study have any value beyond aiding the education of young people? Do all philosophers deserve to be beaten?[3]

Having discussed the nature of philosophy in chapter one, we next ask why philosophy is important. This chapter discusses the importance of philosophy in general. The next chapter addresses the question of the importance of philosophy specifically for Christians. Before attempting to answer the question, it is necessary to clarify what it is asking.

---

[1]Plato, *Gorgias*, in *The Collected Works of Plato*, ed. Edith Hamilton and Huntington Cairns (Princeton, NJ: Princeton University Press, 1961), p. 267.

[2]Ibid., p. 268.

[3]The fantasy of many of my students.

DEVELOPING THE PHILOSOPHICAL MINDSET

In asking, "Why is philosophy important?" we could be asking, "Why is it important to take a course in philosophy in college?" or "Why is it important to know the teachings of major philosophical thinkers and movements?" or "Why is it important to develop a philosophy of life?" Although those are interesting and important questions, the question we are addressing is, Why is it important to develop a philosophical mindset?

A philosophical mindset is an attitude or approach to life that involves regularly examining beliefs to ascertain what they mean, whether they are true and what value they have. It might involve taking a course or reading philosophers, but it is more than these activities. It is adopting a new habit as a way of life. This small book goes beyond presenting the reader with knowledge about philosophy. It is intended to affect nothing less than the manner in which the reader regularly thinks about life.

Living in the information age, we are daily bombarded with new ideas and concepts from films, television programs, music, journalism, advertisements, magazines and books, as well as teachers, ministers, friends and family. Each of these is vying for our attention and attempting to persuade and influence our beliefs, which in turn influence our actions and our worldview. At times these messages are direct and straightforward. More often they are subtle or deeply embedded in our culture and comprise what sociologist Peter Berger calls the "plausibility structures" of society. As a result we often adopt beliefs without much reflection, not realizing how vulnerable to criticism they may be. A philosophical mindset approaches new information critically. It involves questioning, reflecting on and considering the meaning, value and truthfulness of what we see, read or hear.

To adopt a philosophical mindset is to recognize that philosophy is not merely an academic activity within a college course. For many people that may be where they begin to hone their philosophical skills, but it is only the starting point. Nor is thinking philosophically limited to learning what other philosophers have said about certain topics and issues. Reading the great philosophers is an important aspect of studying philosophy, but it is only one aspect. Ultimately thinking philosophically entails a specific approach to life.

As an analogy, consider the difference between a job and an occupational vocation. During my college years I often had to work during summers to make money. I remember several summers I worked as a shipping clerk for an industrial manufacturer. It was just a job, something I did to pay the bills. As a Christian, I did my job faithfully as unto the Lord (Col 3:23). But it was not what I felt called to do with my life. In contrast, I was going to college because I wanted to be a teacher. That was my chosen occupational vocation. I am not a teacher just to make money; I am a teacher because it is where I believe my talents and gifts can best be used. Teaching for me is a deep part of who I am. In this sense, a job is a task performed in order to receive compensation. In the sense I am using "job" here, it is not usually something individuals are tied to in any personal way, and it usually does not affect persons in any deep manner. In contrast, a vocation is a way of life to which persons are called. They may be compensated for performing their vocation, but they are not in it for the money. It is part of who they are; it forms an important part of their identity.[4]

Taking a philosophy course in college can be seen as analogous to a job. You might be in it for the grade or to fulfill a course requirement. However, adopting the philosophical mindset is analogous to accepting the call to a vocation. It is to accept the call to radically change your approach to life. It becomes a part of your identity. To adopt the philosophical mindset is to become a philosopher. Although there are those who work as philosophers (usually through teaching in universities, publishing philosophical books and articles and the like), any person can adopt the vocation of philosopher. Doing so begins by adopting the philosophical mindset. The primary goal of this book is to convert you to becoming a philosopher. If it is successful, you will be a different person from who you were before reading it.[5]

Why is developing such a mindset important? There are many reasons, but we will look at five.

---

[4]The term "vocation" comes from the idea of being called (*voca*, "to call"). None of this is to say that you might not be called to be a shipping clerk or that you should not always do all of your work as to the Lord (Col 3:23). But it is draw a distinction between a doing something only to earn money and doing it as part of fulfilling your life plan.

[5]I realize many readers may have already adopted the philosophical way of life. The fact that you are reading a book on philosophy may be evidence of that.

THE EXAMINED LIFE

Philosophers recognize the value of examining and evaluating core beliefs for a number of reasons. Remember the quote by Socrates? "The unexamined life is not worth living." As was noted in the chapter one, Socrates viewed a human being as the rational animal whose very nature is to reason and reflect. For Socrates, to live the unexamined life is to live a less-than-fully-human life. Therefore, he saw the task of critical examination as an epistemic obligation for all human beings. The term *epistemic* has to do with knowledge and understanding. To say we have an epistemic obligation is the normative claim that we have a duty to clarify our beliefs and be able to offer good reasons for thinking they are true. Many philosophers follow Socrates in holding that we have epistemic obligations concerning what we claim to know. This may not apply to all our beliefs, but it applies to a large number of them.[6]

Examining and evaluating our beliefs, however, is more than fulfilling a duty. It also yields significant dividends, two of which stand out. First, understanding life enhances our enjoyment of it. Contrary to the claim that "ignorance is bliss," wisdom and understanding provide more enduring joy than ignorance.

Think of joy as the fulfillment of an appetite. An appetite is a desire for some object or activity, and the fulfillment of an appetite, especially if the appetite is a good and healthy one, usually produces contentment and joy. Although some appetites are artificially induced, there are a number of natural appetites. Many of these are physical appetites that we share with other members of the animal kingdom: hunger, thirst, rest and sex.

As humans we also experience a number of nonphysical appetites. For example, we have a social appetite that is fulfilled through significant relationships with friends and family. We have an aesthetic appetite fulfilled through our experience of beauty in the world, such as the joy of observing a marvelous sunset, hearing a beautiful piece of music or reading a great story. Humans also have an existential appetite: a desire for meaning and purpose. As Christians we believe the exis-

[6]Many philosophers hold that some beliefs, called basic beliefs, do not require justification and yet we are still warranted in maintaining such beliefs. This view is called externalism and will be discussed briefly in chapter four. This does not discount the need to critically examine such beliefs.

tential appetite is ultimately satisfied only in relationship with God. "Our hearts are restless until they find their rest in thee," Augustine prayed.[7] Although we experience only glimmers and glimpses of such rest and joy in this world, its ultimate manifestation comes in the experience of the beatific vision when our joy will be complete. All these are distinctly human appetites, and most would agree that they are often more important than the physical appetites that we share with non-human animals. Who hasn't had the experience of sacrificing sleep to spend a little more time with good friends or enjoy a good book?

One of these nonphysical appetites is our intellectual appetite: a natural desire to know and understand. This appetite is so powerful that we are often frustrated when we do not understand a concept or idea. Many of us can recall being in a class where the teacher was explaining a particularly complex concept and we were confused or lost. We struggled to understand but did not seem to seem to grasp it, and so we experienced feelings of frustration and inadequacy. Then all of a sudden the teacher made a comment, the light bulb suddenly went on, and it all came together. We might have even felt a physical rush of exhilaration and exclaimed, "Oh, now I get it!" That joyous feeling was our intellectual appetite being fulfilled.

Let me share a personal experience. I was originally a music major in college and had to take several courses in music theory and history. I remember having to study opera and not particularly relishing the prospect. In fact, the idea of listening to opera sickened me. Ample ladies screeching at the top of their lungs in a foreign language was not exactly my idea of a pleasant experience. But as I started to study opera, the history of how operas developed, how they are structured, the different types of operas and major operatic literature, I began to develop an appreciation for operas and could enjoy them. Now, don't get me wrong. I do not come home every night and listen to *La Boheme* or go around humming Wagner. However, I did come to enjoy opera more than I ever thought I would because I gained a basic knowledge and understanding of it. The same is true of understanding our core beliefs about life. We can come to a deeper appreciation of life if we understand it better. Philosophy aids in understanding life better.

[7]Augustine, *Confessions*, bk. 1, chap. 1, trans. F. J. Sheed (Indianapolis: Hackett, 1970), p. 3.

A second benefit to examining and evaluating our foundational beliefs becomes apparent when we consider how strongly our beliefs affect us. Most of our actions originate out of our beliefs, and we often will act on a belief whether it is true or not. One bright summer day while I was working in my yard I stepped into my shed to get a shovel. As I was looking for it I glanced over in the corner and saw a snake curled up ready to strike. At that moment I did what any brave-hearted American male would do: I ran out of the shed as fast as I could. Summoning up my courage in an attempt to salvage some dignity, I grabbed a rake and slowly sneaked back into the shed only to find that what I thought was a snake turned out to be a hank of rope curled up on the floor. As convinced as I was it had been a snake, on reflection I realized that coming into a dark shed from the brightness of the day, I misperceived the rope and imaginatively put a snake in its place. Even though my initial belief was wrong, I still acted and felt as if it was true. Such is the tremendous power of our beliefs.

The power of our core beliefs is much stronger. Most of our beliefs are built on one another. As we move down this structure of justification we get closer to our foundational or core beliefs. We might act on the basis of a particular belief at the top of the pyramid, but the ultimate reason is often justified by a belief much farther down the pyramid. Peter Singer, the endowed chair in bioethics at Princeton University's Center for Human Values, is a well-known advocate of infanticide (the killing of severely deformed newborns). He justifies this by an appeal to utilitarian calculations as he understands them. If the aggregate happiness in the world would be greater if a child were not alive, then we are justified in killing her. Singer adopts utilitarianism for a number of reasons, but a primary one is his acceptance of Darwinian evolution.[8] Darwinian evolution is the idea that humans evolved purely through unguided naturalistic selection without the intervention of an intelligent being. Singer is also a materialist who denies final and formal causality. So Singer's ultimate justification for killing deformed infants derives in

[8]Singer discusses the relationship of his bioethics to Darwinian evolution in *Writings on an Ethical Life* (New York: Ecco Press, 2001), pp. 77-78, 220-21. He specifically comments on how, on his reading, Darwin desanctified human life, placing all life on the same level.

part from an important foundational belief: Is reality directed by a divine, intelligent being who imbues it with meaning, purpose and value, or is reality blindly evolving on its own with no real value, meaning or purpose?[9] Our foundational beliefs affect almost every area of our lives. It is thus vital to take the time and effort to examine and evaluate them to ensure that they are correct.

Examining and evaluating our beliefs fulfills our epistemic duties, makes life more joyful by satisfying our intellectual appetites and pays proper recognition to the powerful effect our beliefs have on our actions and emotions.

CLARIFICATION

One afternoon a few years ago I was sitting in my office when a student came by to see me. She was upset over the grade she received on a recent exam. Her opening comment to me was, "I think your tests are unfair." When I asked why she thought that, she said, "I studied for several hours for the last test and ended up with a D. But my roommate, who took the same test, studied for less than an hour and ended up with an A. That's not fair. I studied longer and worked harder than she did. She hardly did anything. I should get the higher grade." There were a number of things we needed to discuss, but part of her problem was a need to clarify the term *fair*.

I explained to her that she was using a quantitative concept of fairness. Under this concept, the quantity of time or effort one puts into a task should determine the reward one receives from it. Those who expend more time and effort should get more than those who expend less time and effort. This is a legitimate concept of fairness in some situations. We often pay wages on this basis: those who work more hours get paid more than those who work fewer hours. I explained, however, that this is not the only way to think of "fair." Another concept of fairness is the qualitative concept. Under this concept it is the quality of one's work that is determinative of the reward one

[9]It is important to note here that I am not suggesting that all who subscribe to Darwinian evolution are advocates of infanticide. Even for Singer, Darwinian evolution appears to be a necessary condition for infanticide but not a sufficient one.

receives. Those whose work is more excellent receive a higher reward than those whose work is inferior. This is also a legitimate concept of fairness in some situations.

Which of these two concepts is appropriate in this situation? I explained to the student that the qualitative concept is appropriate for awarding grades. The primary purpose of education is to achieve a good understanding of content or to gain the ability to employ a skill. Students are awarded superior grades based on the quality of their understanding. I commended her on the amount of time and effort she put into studying, but time and effort alone are not enough to receive a high grade. We then went on to discuss ways she could better understand the material and achieve a higher grade on the next test.

This illustrates another value of developing a philosophical mindset: it aids in the task of clarification. Philosophers consider clarification to be important in two respects. First, it is important that we are clear about what we believe for our own benefit. Our actions, motivations and feelings are predicated on our beliefs, which means we need to be clear about what those beliefs are.

Second, clarifying terms and concepts is of utmost importance because our discussions with others about our beliefs are based on a shared understanding of what those terms and concepts mean. That is why most well-written philosophical literature begins with an explanation and definition of terms and ideas. The author wants to make sure that he and his readers are on the same page immediately. Consider this example from the opening paragraphs of Richard Taylor's discussion of determinism in his book on metaphysics:

Reflections such as this suggest that, in the case of everything that exists, there are antecedent conditions, known or unknown, which, because they are given, mean that things could not be other than they are. This is an exact statement of the metaphysical thesis of *determinism*. More loosely, it says that everything, including every cause, is the effect of some cause or causes; or that everything is not only determinate but causally determined.[10]

[10]Richard Taylor, *Metaphysics*, 2nd ed. (Englewood Cliffs, NJ: Prentice-Hall, 1974), p. 39.

When entering a philosophical discussion, it is important to make sure that all participants are clear on the meaning of the terms involved. If they are not, they end up wasting time in fruitless discussion. Oftentimes when I begin a discussion of determinism in class, students think I am talking about the theological issue of predestination. Predestination is the belief that an all-loving and knowing God predetermined events in the world. However, as Taylor's definition makes clear, determinism does not entail the involvement of any such being.[11] Events occur purely on the basis of antecedent conditions and prior causes, whatever those may be. So I take the time to carefully spell out exactly what it is we are talking about.

I once read a debate in the newspaper between two individuals on the topic of euthanasia. One person was strongly against it; the other believed it was justifiable at times. As I closely read their arguments it occurred to me that these two agreed more than they disagreed. Their disagreement was mostly a merely apparent one and was due to the fact that they did not define what they meant by euthanasia. The individual who opposed it thought of euthanasia as mercy killing, taking action that would hasten the death of a patient. The individual who thought it was sometimes justifiable spoke of disconnecting patients from machines that were keeping them alive and allowing nature to take its course. These are two different concepts of euthanasia. The first is often referred to as active euthanasia, while the latter is called passive euthanasia. From my reading of the debate, I came to believe that both parties were in agreement that active euthanasia is not morally permissible, but that, under some conditions, passive euthanasia would be appropriate. The two participants might have saved a lot of ink if they had taken the time to clarify what they meant by euthanasia. This is the importance of clarification.

The Value of Arguing

If philosophy is the pursuit for the truth, then arguing is the strategy that guides that pursuit. Philosophers love to argue and do so all the time. In fact, arguing is their primary task. They construct arguments,

---

[11]It is true that predestination is sometimes referred to as a subcategory of determinism called theological determinism. This is because of the fact that, although determinism does not entail predestination, certain forms of predestination do entail some form of determinism.

evaluate the arguments of others and produce counterarguments against those arguments. However, in order to understand this task, we need to clarify what we mean by "argue."

Many people do not like arguing. They picture an angry dispute between two individuals. Most of us have been involved in this kind of argument. It is usually characterized by negative emotions: we are upset, raise our voices and maybe even stomp out of the room in frustration. In this kind of argument we usually attack the opposing person: "You're mean," "You're irresponsible and insensitive." We cast the other person as the bad person: she is the problem, and if she would just get her act together, everything would be fine. Usually, if we are honest, the goal of this kind of argument is to win: to show her that I am right and she is wrong. Because these arguments are such negative experiences, we try to avoid them as much as possible.

Another type of arguing features a dispute not between competing individuals but between competing ideas. This is the kind of arguing philosophers do. Rather than being emotional, it is rational.[12] We are seeking reasons for why we think a belief is true. In arguing this way, we do not attack the other person, but we are both attacking an issue or problem. This is why philosophers often can hold opposite views on issues and yet be good friends. The goal of this kind of arguing is not to win but to find the truth. In fact, if you can show me that a belief I had thought was true is actually false, I have not lost but have won, because I do not want to hold a false belief and am now closer to the truth. Rather than avoiding this kind of arguing, philosophers encourage it.

Arguing is so important in philosophy because it is the foremost way that we fulfill the justification aspect of critical examination. To justify our beliefs is to offer reasons for why we think they are true. When we offer those reasons we are presenting an argument. There are right ways to argue and wrong ways to argue, so we need guidelines on how to argue correctly. Because this is so important to philosophy, the second half of this book will discuss such guidelines.

[12]This is not meant to imply that philosophers are complete stoics. They can become passionate in offering their arguments because they deeply believe in them. However, the basis for their argument is not emotional but rational.

Another value of arguing philosophically is that it forces us to understand an issue better. In arguing we strip an issue down to its basic elements, clarify what we mean and provide reasons for our beliefs about it. Socrates is an excellent model of this. In the dialogues of Plato, Socrates often confronts a citizen of Athens by questioning him about what he believes or what he is doing. The citizen is forced to think through the belief or activity and present arguments as answers to Socrates's questions, a method that did not earn Socrates any popularity awards. This is called the Socratic method, and it is still often employed in education. It is the primary method used in law school. Teachers require students to present arguments in class not because the teacher needs proof but to make sure that the student understands what he is talking about.

CULTIVATING A WORLDVIEW

One of the greatest values of the philosophical mindset is the significant role it plays in helping us to cultivate a comprehensive system by which our knowledge can be categorized and examined. This is called a worldview. A worldview can be defined as an explanation and interpretation of the world and an application of that view to life.

Let us take an event and compare two different worldviews concerning how one might respond to it. On December 26, 2004, a 9.0 magnitude earthquake occurred about 100 miles off the coast of Indonesia. This earthquake caused a series of tsunamis to hit along the coastline of the Indian Ocean and resulted in the deaths of 280,000 persons and the displacement of more than 3 million additional persons who lost their homes and livelihoods.

How people respond to such an event depends greatly on their worldview. A Christian might respond first by wondering why God would allow such a tragedy to take place. He might never know why but is convinced that God, in his infinite love and wisdom, often has purposes beyond what we can see. He might also wonder about the salvation of those lost and would pray for the well-being of the survivors. Many Christians would reach out in Christian charity and attempt to provide aid to the survivors.

A confirmed atheist would probably also sympathize with those who suffered. She too might reach out and help.[13] But she will not wonder why God allows such tragedies to occur, because there is no God. She might say there is no real explanation for why things like this happen. In fact, this event may confirm her in her atheism. She might ask, "How could one believe in a loving God who allows such tragedies to occur?"[14] She will not pray for anyone, as she believes there is no one to pray to. She will not wonder about an individual's salvation because, according to her worldview, there is no afterlife in which people experience salvation. The contrast here between the Christian and atheist illustrates how each person's worldview affects the response to life's events.

Although everyone holds a worldview, not everyone has done the real labor of cultivating a worldview. Some people adopt, without much critical reflection, their worldview by accepting what they were told or what their culture proclaims or tacitly endorses. To cultivate a worldview is to reflect on our foundational beliefs, to consider the different options concerning them and to arrive at a good justification for holding the beliefs we do. There are three elements to consider in cultivating a worldview.

First, the beliefs involved in a worldview need to be internally consistent. They should not contradict one another. As an example, examine the following list of beliefs that make up the Christian worldview:[15]

---

[13]It would be wrong to characterize atheists as uncaring or unethical individuals. Most atheists are ethically decent human beings who have compassion for those who are suffering and often reach out to those in need.

[14]At the time of this event I was asked by an atheist how I can believe in God in the face of such a tragedy. My answer was that I need God in order to recognize it as tragic. If atheistic naturalism is correct and there is no God, it is hard to see where value ultimately comes from. In such a valueless universe, there are no tragic events, just events. Humans would have no more value than other life forms, and I did not see anyone mourning over all the bugs that were killed in the tsunamis. Although the atheist might be just as sympathetic as the Christian, even responding in aid, he has a more difficult time, in my view, justifying the value of human beings than does the theist.

[15]By referring to *"the Christian worldview"* I do not mean to imply that there is only one Christian worldview or that all Christians hold all beliefs in common. Within Christianity there are a variety of beliefs and much disagreement over many of those beliefs. However, we can demarcate those core beliefs that are the core essential salient features that distinguish Christianity from other religious and nonreligious worldviews. There is room for some disagreement, but the list of beliefs is one that the vast majority of Christians would identify as salient features of any worldview that would call itself Christian.

a. God exists.
b. God is omnipotent.
c. God is omnibenevolent.
d. God created me.
e. Jesus Christ is God.
f. Jesus loves me.
g. Jesus died for my salvation.
h. Life is meaningless.

It should be immediately apparent that there is something incorrect about this list of beliefs. If *a-g* are accepted as true, then *h* does not belong. An all-loving and all-powerful God would not create a meaningless life, nor would Jesus die for a meaningless life. The set of beliefs above is inconsistent.

Philosophers insist that inconsistency is a sign that something is wrong within a given set of beliefs and that we must make a change to remove the inconsistency. The question is, What do we change? Do we change *h* to bring it in line with *a-g*? Or do we change *a-g* to bring them in line with *h*? This is not as easy to decide as we might first think. Our initial response might be to change *h* because it is easier to change one belief than six other beliefs, but the number of beliefs is not always relevant. Thomas Kuhn argues that a whole paradigm shift in a person's worldview might occur on the basis of one new fact coming to light.[16] When Copernicus discovered that the earth goes around the sun, instead of the other way around, it changed not only astronomy but affected social, philosophical and theological ideas as well.

The question of what to change depends on which beliefs have the best support in their favor. Many Christians would argue in favor of changing *h* and bringing it in line with *a-g*. However, at times some Christians who are encountering extremely difficult circumstances are tempted to give up *a-g* because at that moment *h* might have more subjective force. I have spoken with Christians who have lost their children to illness or accident. Their grief is so incredibly unbearable I cannot even begin to imagine what they are going through. They raise their angry fists to God and

---

[16]Thomas Kuhn, *The Structure of Scientific Revolutions*, 3rd ed. (Chicago: University of Chicago Press, 1996).

scream, "Why did you allow my child to go through this?" Their perception is that all they get in reply is silence. For many of these Christians, the idea that life is meaningless becomes more real to them at that moment than all those seemingly empty and void theological pronouncements about God. Unless one is firmly established in one's worldview, a tragic event can severely challenge it and in some cases may cause one to abandon it altogether. Ensuring internal consistency is a crucial step to cultivating and defending a worldview. Those of us who are well established in our Christian worldview recognize that because we believe that *a–g* are true, then *h* should be changed to

h¹: Life is meaningful.

The fact that God loves me and that Jesus died for me encourages me to hold that life is meaningful, a conviction that can sustain me when I encounter difficult times. I do not have to bear my burden alone.

A second aspect of a worldview is external comprehensiveness. Comprehensive does not mean that every single belief has to be accounted for by our worldview. It means instead that when a new fact that might have a profound effect on a worldview comes to light, the worldview needs to account for it. Consider the worldview above (incorporating the new *h¹*):

a. God exists.
b. God is omnipotent.
c. God is omnibenevolent.
d. God created me.
e. Jesus Christ is God.
f. Jesus loves me.
g. Jesus died for my salvation.
h¹. Life is meaningful.

Let us now add a new belief:

i. Evil exists.

For many it might appear that we again have an inconsistent set. Some might claim, "If God is omnipotent (all-powerful), then he can do away with evil, and if he is omnibenevolent (all-good), then he would desire to be rid of evil. So why is there evil? The existence of evil is inconsistent with an all-good and an all-powerful God." This is known as the problem of evil, and for many atheists it is the primary reason they reject any belief in God, at least the God of classical theism.

As we noted above, internal consistency is a hallmark of a solid worldview, but in this case it is difficult to know what to do. We cannot deny the existence of evil in the world. It is obvious that evil occurs either through the actions of persons who choose to do such evil or through natural events such as diseases and disasters. Yet orthodox theists do not want to deny the basic theological truths of God's omnipotence or omnibenevolence either.

Whatever we decide in this case, philosophy insists that we cannot ignore the issue and pretend it is not there. Philosophy also frowns on those who want to claim it is a mystery or a paradox that we cannot explain.[17] This is too important a challenge to our worldview to let the inconsistency remain unresolved. If evil exists, then we need to account for it in our worldview. This is one of the real values of adopting the philosophical mindset: it plays a significant role in reflecting on conundrums like this. Many Christian philosophers have written extensively on the problem of evil and have shown that one can believe in both the existence of evil and the existence of an omnipotent and omnibenevolent God without any inconsistency.[18]

We regularly encounter new information that may challenge our worldview. When we do, the philosophical mindset requires that we account for it. This might involve showing how the new information fits within our worldview. This is what many Christian philosophers offer concerning the problem of evil. At other times it may involve

---

[17]This is not to deny that there are some aspects of God that we have difficulty explaining. But it is saying that we have an obligation to at least try to reconcile competing beliefs, especially on such an important issue. Pushing the "mystery button" too soon is an expression of intellectual cowardice, and treating contradictions as mere tensions or antinomies is dishonest. This is also not to say that we always know why God allows certain specific evils and suffering to occur. There are times when we need to trust that he has reasons we may never be aware of.

[18]For some modern works dealing with the problem of evil, see William Hasker, *The Triumph of God Over Evil: Theodicy for a World of Suffering* (Downers Grove, IL: InterVarsity Press, 2008); Norman L. Geisler, *The Roots of Evil* (Eugene, OR: Wipf and Stock, 2002); John S. Feinberg, *The Many Faces of Evil: Theological Systems and the Problem of Evil* (Wheaton, IL: Crossway, 2004); and Alvin Plantinga, *God, Freedom and Evil* (Grand Rapids: Eerdmans, 1977).

adapting our worldview to the new information; none of us should be so committed to a worldview that we are not willing to change our minds if that is where the evidence leads. Sometimes a new idea will force us to reexamine our worldview and to make significant changes because the veracity of the new idea is so overwhelming. For many years Antony Flew was arguably the most famous atheist in the world. He had published dozens of articles and books arguing against the validity of believing in God and debated many theists on the issue. As a philosopher he was committed to the principle of following the evidence where it leads. He believed that the evidence did not lead to belief in a God. Then, a few years ago, he was confronted with evidence that compelled him to acknowledge that the universe is the product of an intelligent designer, which called for a complete reevaluation of his basic worldview. He announced he had become a theist at a symposium in 2004. When asked if the thought intelligence was involved in the origin of life, he said:

Yes, I now think it does . . . almost entirely because of the DNA investigations. What I think the DNA material has done is that it has shown, by the almost unbelievable complexity of the arrangements which are needed to produce [life], that intelligence must have been involved in getting these extraordinary diverse elements to work together. It's the enormous complexity of the number of elements and the enormous subtlety of the ways they work together. The meeting of these two parts at the right time by chance is simply minute. It is all a matter of the enormous complexity by which the results were achieved, which looked to me like the work of intelligence.[19]

The third element of a worldview is coherence. The beliefs involved in a worldview should fit together and mutually support one another. A worldview is not merely a loose collection of beliefs. It is a set of related beliefs that together form a basis from which to act in the world. Note the following set of beliefs:

j. Virginia is a beautiful state.
k. Abraham Lincoln was the sixteenth president of the United States.

[19] Antony Flew, *There Is a God: How the World's Most Notorious Atheist Changed His Mind* (New York: HarperOne, 2007), p. 75. It should be noted that Flew does not consider himself to be a Christian theist. His theism is better thought of as deism at this stage.

l. Pizza is one of America's favorite foods.

m. $a^2 + b^2 = c^2$

n. The half-life of carbon-14 is about 5,730 years.

o. *Casablanca* is a great movie.

This set of beliefs fulfills the first two elements of a worldview. It is internally consistent and arguably externally comprehensive. However, it does not form a worldview. The beliefs are not basic enough to qualify as a worldview, there is no relationship between them, and they do not mutually support one another. There is no coherence. In our previous set, a–h[1], in contrast, the beliefs did mutually support one another. The fact that God loves me and that Jesus is God supports and coheres with the idea that he died for me.

Consistency, comprehensiveness and coherence are facets of every worldview worth its salt. A philosophical mindset is necessary to assure that all three are functioning harmoniously together. Such assurance provides confidence that our worldview is well reasoned and intact.

THE PRACTICAL VALUE OF PHILOSOPHY

There is an old Latin saying: *philosophia panem non torrit*, or "Philosophy bakes no bread." The saying was originally meant to convey that one cannot make any money as a philosopher[20] but has come to mean that philosophy has no practical value. That is how many see philosophical speculation. Many people think philosophy is an activity performed only by academic scholars who sit in ivory towers discussing how many angels can dance on the head of a pin. It does not have anything to do with the day-to-day life of the average person. Part of this is understandable. Sometimes it does seem that philosophical inquiry is far removed from our everyday world. Questions about the nature of reality, whether we are really free or determined, how the mind interacts with the body, how one justifies beliefs and what constitutes art do not relate to our daily lives of paying the bills, fixing the toilet or raising children. Philosophy, though, is more practical than many think.

---

[20] A truism to which I can attest.

First, a person's worldview determines his ultimate goals, and these in turn strongly shape everyday decisions. I once had a conversation after class with a student who did not think philosophy was practical. I asked him, "Why are you taking this class?"

He said, "Well, I have to."

"That is not true," I said. "You don't have to be here. No one is threatening you or forcing you to sit in my class. You are free to leave. So why are you here?"

He replied, "I guess I am here because I want to earn a college degree and this is a required course, so I am taking it to get my degree."

"But why do you want a college degree?" I asked.

"I want eventually to go to law school, and I need to have a college degree to do that," he replied.

"What kind of law do you want to practice?"

He replied, "Business law. That's where the real money is."

"So your goal is to become a lawyer with some big firm and make lots of money so you can buy a nice house, a great car and in general be happy," I summarized.

"Yeah, so how does philosophy fit in?" he asked.

I then told him, "Suppose I could take a crystal ball and show you the future and it turns out none of that will happen—that this path will not lead to the fulfillment and happiness you desire. If that were true, then it seems you would question why you are here, taking this class right now. It's not going to result in what you want, and you should be out finding the path that will get you what you ultimately want. That is thinking philosophically."[21]

Today's choices will mold tomorrow. Philosophy helps us consider what our goals for the future should be and how to best achieve them. An old proverb states that we should understand life backward but live it forward. There is wisdom in the idea that a person should look at the end of her life, decide what she wants to have accomplished and then, thinking backwards from the end, plan out her life. It is similar to

---

[21]We also discussed how the law is a philosophically oriented discipline involving sophisticated and complex reasoning skills. Few undergraduate-level courses could be more relevant to preparing for law school than philosophy.

solving a maze. Most people know that if you start at the beginning and work forward there is a good chance of taking a wrong turn and getting lost. However, if you start at the end and go backward, the way out is usually much clearer. Start at the end of life and ask yourself, "What do I want to have written on my gravestone? What do I want people to say about me at my funeral?" Whatever that is, mentally trace your life backwards, noting each step you need to take to get to that ultimate goal. Once you have it mapped out in this backwards manner, begin living it forward by taking those steps. You should also expect that you may have to adjust your map to account for the contingencies that life often throws your way. The project of thinking about goals, planning out life and making adjustments is a philosophical endeavor.

There is another way to see the relationship of philosophy to daily life. I once heard someone say, "The quality of your life is largely dependent on the daily choices you make. So choose wisely." There is much truth here. We often think that the most important choices we make are the big ones: whom we marry, where we go to college or what career we choose to follow. Although these are important, they tend to overshadow other choices that are often equally, if not more, important. These are the regular, daily choices we make in our interactions with others and in our private lives. These choices form our character and reflect and influence our worldview. Should I tell the truth in this situation? Which activity should I invest my time in today? What does it mean to be a faithful friend? We make character-forming decisions like these on a daily basis, and our character is built over a lifetime of small decisions. A philosophical mindset is necessary to help us think wisely about these choices. Choosing wisely is what philosophy is all about, and what could be of greater practical importance than that? Ed Miller and Jon Jensen put it this way:

A moment's thought reveals that the questions that may seem to be the most remote are also the most important. What we think about our own selves, God, the physical universe, value, and the like—and, as we just insisted, we all *do* think about these things—determines how we actually live in the world. . . . If you doubt this, a little reflection on your activities, commitments, aspirations, and decisions this very day will probably prove it.[22]

Some claim, "But the quality of my life isn't always up to me. Sometimes things happen to us outside our control." Yes, but we decide how to respond to those things. We can choose to respond wisely, learning from such things and growing through them, or we can choose to respond in bitterness and resentment. Joni Tada Erickson is an example of the former. She was involved in a swimming accident in which she became a quadriplegic. For two years she was miserable and bitter, even contemplating suicide. But with the help of therapy and the support of a community of believers, she chose to respond to her situation with a firm conviction to make good of it. The result is that she became a world-renowned artist and author, ministering to others who are disabled. We choose how to respond, and we should choose wisely. That is the practicality of philosophy.

A second practical function of philosophy is the role it plays when individuals evaluate questions and problems in other fields. No matter what discipline one is in, whether it is business, psychology or science, one will eventually encounter basic philosophical questions. J. P. Moreland offers a few examples:

A biblical exegete becomes aware of how much her own cultural background shapes what she can see in the biblical text, and she begins to wonder whether meaning might not reside in the interpretation and not the text itself . . .

A psychologist reads the literature regarding identical twins who are reared in separate environments. He notes that they usually exhibit similar adult behavior. He then wonders if there is really any such thing as freedom of the will, and if not, he ponders what to make of moral responsibility and punishment . . .

A neurophysiologist cultivates specific correlations between certain brain functions and certain feelings of pain, and she puzzles over whether or not there is a soul or mind distinct from the brain . . .

A businessman notices the government is not adequately caring for

[22]Ed L. Miller and Jon Jensen, *Questions That Matter: An Introduction to Philosophy*, 6th ed. (New York: McGraw-Hill, 2009), p. 29.

the poor. He discusses with a friend the issue of whether or not businesses have corporate moral responsibilities or whether only individuals have moral responsibilities . . .

An education major is asked to state his philosophy of education. In order to do this he must state his views on human nature, the nature of truth, how people learn, what roles values play in the life, what the purpose of education ought to be and who should be entitled to an education.[23]

Medical practice regularly involves philosophical questions about the nature of reality (What is a person, and when does personhood begin? Do we maintain personal identity even when we are in the advanced stages of Alzheimer's disease?), knowledge claims (What are the necessary and sufficient criteria for knowing a person is dead?) and moral values (Is a physician justified in lying to his patient if it will maintain the patient's welfare?).

Philosophy even plays a role in casual activities like sports. Consider the following questions: What is the difference between a sport and a game? What, if any, are the necessary and sufficient conditions for an activity to qualify as a sport? If sports are defined by their constituent rules, can cheaters ever win or, by not keeping the rules and hence not really playing the game, do they only appear to win? Is the beauty of the sport an objective quality or a purely subjective one? Should we evaluate the true fan by his loyalty to a particular team even when they are performing poorly, or is the true fan of the sport one who honors it by being loyal to whichever team is the best at that moment? At the foundation of every activity reside philosophical questions.

One of the most common ways that philosophy is practical is the role it plays in our ethical reasoning. We regularly make moral decisions. Sometimes these are small and trivial, like keeping a commitment to mow the lawn instead of playing tennis. Other moral decisions can be major and life-changing: whether to keep a loved one on life support or remove the support and allow that person to die. Not only do we ponder the ethical decisions in our own lives,

---

[23]J. P. Moreland, "Philosophy," in *Opening the American Mind*, ed. W. David Beck (Grand Rapids: Baker, 1991), pp. 58-59.

but also we are often confronted with social and cultural issues that involve moral decisions. Is capital punishment ever justified? As Christians, how should we think about participating in war? Should we support businesses that exploit the poor in other countries? Should gay marriage be legalized?

Whatever we decide, whether the issue is personal or social, we need good reasons. This process of finding moral justification for our choices involves thinking philosophically. How do we decide what is right and what is wrong? At first we might appeal to some moral rule or principle that we have adopted, but the process does not end there, for the rule itself begs for justification. We justify our moral rules by appealing to an overarching moral theory that governs all our moral justification. For some, it is the consequences of our actions that control our moral decisions. If the results of our decisions are good, then they are deemed morally justified. So, if lying to someone will bring about a good result, then lying becomes permissible. If helping a terminal patient commit suicide ends his suffering, then assisted suicide is thought morally justified. For others, it is not the consequences that make an action right or wrong; instead, certain actions are regarded intrinsically right or wrong regardless of the results. Immanuel Kant believed that an action is right only if it expresses the good will: doing it because it is our duty, not because of what it produces. Hastening the death of human beings on this analysis may well be considered wrong because human beings are intrinsically valuable.[24] Or a Kantian might think lying is wrong because truth has intrinsic value regardless of the results and therefore one has a duty to tell the truth.

Then there are those who appeal neither to consequences nor to moral duties but instead to character qualities called virtues in making moral decisions. A moral virtue is a dispositional trait built into our character. For the virtue thinker, our actions flow out of our character. Rather than thinking in terms of duties, virtue ethicists try to determine which actions are appropriate expressions of certain virtues such as love,

---

[24]Many Christians argue that our intrinsic value arises from our being made in the image of God. When a person murders a fellow human being, it is an affront to God himself (see Gen 9:6).

loyalty or integrity. These individuals often make moral decisions by attempting to model morally ideal persons. They might ask, "What would _____ do if he were faced with this decision?"[25] There are even those who think morality is completely relative and needs no justification because it is up to each person to decide what is right or wrong based purely on individual desires or preferences.

Whatever moral theory a person might adopt, the justification process does not necessarily stop there. Ultimately she might need to appeal to her entire worldview to justify her moral theory. Every step of reflective moral thinking involves the philosophical mindset.

Another practical value of philosophy concerns how we relate with one another. As we noted above, one task of philosophy is cultivating and understanding worldviews. There are a variety of worldviews held by different individuals. Understanding another's worldview, knowing its basic presuppositions and where he is coming from, aids in the task of relating to him. Understanding one another is the basis for fruitful dialogue, mutual respect and tolerance. We might not agree on the worldview level, but philosophy helps us live and work together as we find ways to respectfully talk about our disagreements. The more we understand philosophy, the better we understand each other.

Finally, philosophy is practical in the way that it opens and expands our minds to new ideas and options we may have never considered. It helps to rid us of dogmatism, prejudice and poor reasoning. We become more critical (i.e., analytical) of what we read, see and hear. We are assailed daily with new ideas, and we need to evaluate them critically before we accept them. All too often we allow our presuppositions to control what we accept without taking the time to ask, What really is meant here? Do I have reason to believe it is true?

One of the most well-known philosophers of the twentieth century, Bertrand Russell, thought this was the greatest benefit of philosophy. He wrote:

The man who has no tincture of philosophy goes through life imprisoned in the prejudices derived from common sense, from the habitual beliefs of his age or his nation, and from convictions which have grown up in his mind without the co-operation or consent of his deliberate reason. To such a man the world tends to become definite, finite, obvious; common objects rouse no questions, and unfamiliar possibilities are contemptuously rejected. As soon as we begin to philosophize, on the contrary, we find, as we saw in our opening chapters, that even the most everyday things lead to problems. . . . Philosophy, though unable to tell us with certainty what is the true answer to the doubts which it raises, is able to suggest many possibilities which enlarge our thoughts and free them from the tyranny of custom. Thus, while diminishing our feeling of certainty as to what things are, it greatly increases our knowledge as to what they may be; it removes the somewhat arrogant dogmatism of those who have never travelled into the region of liberating doubt, and it keeps alive our sense of wonder by showing familiar things in an unfamiliar aspect... philosophy has a value—perhaps its chief value—through the greatness of the objects which it contemplates, and the freedom from narrow and personal aims resulting from this contemplation.[26]

Philosophy awakens us from of our dogmatic slumbers (to pilfer a phrase from Kant). It opens our minds to new options and ideas. It is the primary means of intellectual and spiritual growth. It is the love of wisdom. It is not merely wisdom's casual acquaintance or affable friend but passionate lover.

CONCLUSION

We began this chapter by asking whether Callicles was correct in his assessment that philosophy may be helpful as an aid to educating children but otherwise is a waste of time. This chapter has argued that there is value in adopting the philosophical mindset. It is an important element of the nature of human beings to reflect, clarify and seek answers to the most important questions in life. The process of arguing through the varied answers to these questions helps in sharpening our minds and in cultivating and maintaining a consistent worldview. Several examples of the practicality of philosophy were offered to

[26]Bertrand Russell, *The Problems of Philosophy* (1912; Simon and Brown edition, 2010), pp. 109-10.

show that philosophy is not a dusty discipline of academia or arcane habit of intellectuals, but that it vitally affects our daily choices in life in a myriad of ways both obvious and subtle. Philosophy is not just the task of a select few who teach in colleges and universities. It is the calling of every individual to ponder, reflect and argue on the important questions of life, knowledge and values, be they moral, political, social or aesthetic. Philosophy truly is one of those activities that sets us apart from all other created things.

three

WHAT ATHENS HAS TO DO WITH JERUSALEM

The Importance of Philosophy for Christians

A number of years ago I was recommended to a specialist due to problems I was having with my throat. On learning that I taught at a Christian institution, he told me that he is a believer himself. He asked me what I teach, and I told him philosophy. He looked at me sternly and responded, "Philosophy? What is a Christian doing teaching philosophy? Don't you know what the Bible says about philosophy? It says 'Beware of philosophy.' Christians should have nothing to do with philosophy." Suddenly my throat was feeling a lot worse.

I have had similar reactions from nonbelievers. When they find out that I teach philosophy at a Christian university, they often raise their eyebrows and say, "I wouldn't think they would offer philosophy there. Isn't that a Christian school? I wouldn't think Christians would be open to studying philosophy." Such reactions, sadly enough, do not surprise me anymore. But they do raise an important question: What place does the study of philosophy have for Christians? I want to argue that it has an extremely important role to play in the Christian life. In fact, it is a key ingredient to being an effective disciple of Jesus Christ in the world we live in today.

THE BIBLICAL BASIS FOR DEVELOPING A PHILOSOPHICAL MINDSET

A biblical mandate. Christians take Scripture seriously and will often turn there as a starting point for evaluating a particular practice. It may surprise some to discover that the word *philosophy* occurs only once in all of Scripture. At first glance the context appears to be negative, hence the notion that Scripture frowns on philosophy. However, on inspection we realize that Scripture is not condemning philosophy. Just the opposite is the case. It advocates the need for a philosophical mindset. We find the passage in Paul's letter to the Colossians.

Colossae was a town in the Lycus valley of Phrygia. In the fifth century B.C. it had been a large, wealthy city, but by the Christian era it had become a small village due to the growth of two neighboring cities, Laodicea and Hierapolis. From Paul's letter we know that he had never visited the town (Col 2:1), but it was part of his larger evangelistic ministry in nearby Ephesus between A.D. 52 and 55. According to F. F. Bruce, "While the work was directed by Paul, he was assisted by several colleagues, and through their ministry in various parts of the province churches were planted, some of which the apostle was unable to visit personally."[1] One of Paul's colleagues was Epaphras, who apparently was the founder of the church in Colossae and remained as their elder when Paul moved on.

It is now five years later, and Paul is a prisoner in Rome. Epaphras has come to visit Paul and brings news of a heretical teaching that has developed within the church at Colossae. Addressing this heresy is the primary purpose of Paul's letter to the Colossians. Biblical scholars are divided over the exact nature of this heresy. What little we know about it can only be inferred from this letter.[2] As best as can be seen it appears to be a type of Jewish heresy, though not the same as the Judaizing heresy Paul addresses in his letter to the Galatians. From what we can gather, the Colossian heresy instead seems to be a syncretism of Jewish tradition with Hellenistic teaching.

[1] E. K. Simpson and F. F. Bruce, *Commentary on the Epistles to the Ephesians and to the Colossians* (Grand Rapids: Eerdmans, 1957), pp. 163-64.

[2] P. T. O'Brien catalogs five different interpretations of what the precise nature of the heresy might be. His conclusion is that although general characteristics can be garnered through the letter, the origin or specifics of the heresy are open to debate. See P. T. O'Brien, *Colossians and Philemon*, Word Biblical Commentary 44 (Waco, TX: Word, 1982), pp. xxx-xxxvii.

Paul sets up his address against this heresy by affirming the faith and salvation of his audience (Col 1:2-6) and the authoritative ministry of Epaphras in their midst (Col 1:7-8). He assures them of his prayers for their continued growth in "the knowledge of his will in all spiritual wisdom and understanding" (Col 1:9) and their continually bearing fruit "increasing in the knowledge of God" (Col 1:11). These phrases foreshadow the nature of the heresy Paul will address later and contain philosophically key terms: *knowledge, wisdom and understanding*. He transitions into a discussion of the foundation for their faith in one of the great christological passages in all of Scripture (Col 1:15-23), affirming that Christ is the visible image of the invisible God (Col 1:15) through whom all things were made (Col 1:16-17), that he is the head of the church (Col 1:18) and that he has reconciled all things to himself (Col 1:19-23). Paul finishes off this section relating how he is a minister of this gospel to his readers (Col 1:24-2:5).

Having set the stage, Paul now launches into his main message: They are to continue walking in the same faith in which they were established (Col 2:6-7). One important aspect of being established in the faith is the passage we want to center on. It reads as follows: "See to it that no one takes you captive through hollow and deceptive philosophy, which depends on human tradition and elemental spiritual forces [alternate reading: the basic principles] of this world rather than on Christ" (Col 2:8 NIV).

Paul starts this passage with the Greek term *blepete* meaning "beware" or "be on your guard." He then follows this with a strange phrase that literally means "to be carried off as booty" but here is probably more like "kidnap." The means by which the believers can be kidnapped is through "hollow and deceptive philosophy." The literal wording here is "philosophy and vain deceit," but the NIV rendering captures Paul's meaning well. Bruce comments, "In the Greek text *kenēs apatēs* ['vain deceit'] comes under the same regimen as *philosophias* ["philosophy"], and so the 'philosophy' and the 'vain deceit' are the same thing."[3] This hollow and deceptive philosophy is based on "human tradition" and the "basic

---

[3]Simpson and Bruce, *Commentary on the Epistles*, p. 231n28.

principles of the world."[4] It is contrasted against another philosophy, one that is based on Christ. Paul already has detailed the foundational principles of the philosophy based on Christ (Col 1:15-23) as that by which they would continue to grow in "the knowledge of his will in all spiritual wisdom and understanding."

Knowing the historical and literary context of this passage makes clear that Paul is not condemning philosophy in general. He is contrasting two kinds of philosophy: one that is based on "human tradition" and the "basic principles of the world" and another that is based on Christ. He instructs the Colossians (and by way of application, the church as a whole) to beware of being kidnapped by the former and instead to cling to the latter. I call this the biblical mandate to develop a Christian philosophical mindset and want to suggest that this mandate involves three elements: appreciation of the role reasoning plays in evaluating philosophies, construction of a Christian system of philosophy and refutation of contrary philosophies. Each of these requires the philosophical mindset. Let us look at each in detail.

Three elements involved in fulfilling the biblical mandate. First, in order to fulfill Paul's mandate we need to appreciate the value Scripture places on the use of our reason and intellect. In much of the modern church, the opposite view is the case. Many contemporary Christians devalue the use of reason. Much of this is due to the post-Enlightenment view of the dichotomy between faith and reason. It is often asserted that religion is about faith, not reason. It is not surprising that this view is pervasive among secular thinkers, but it has been adopted by many in the modern church. Many Christians have an exaggerated view of human depravity claiming that the noetic effects of sin have so darkened the mind as to be incapable of knowing any truth. Human ability to reason was not just damaged but was destroyed. These Christians believe that to be a truly spiritual person is to have the faith of a child (Mt 18:5). Oftentimes Christians will portray ignorance and foolishness as virtues, quoting passages such as 1 Corinthians 1:18-20:

---

[4]This phrase, translated literally as "elements of the cosmos," appears three times in Paul's letters (Col 2:8, 20; Gal 4:3). There has been much speculation as to its specific meaning. See O'Brien, *Colossians and Philemon,* pp. 129-32.

For the word of the cross is foolishness to those who are perishing, but to us who are being saved it is the power of God. For it is written,

"I WILL DESTROY THE WISDOM OF THE WISE,
AND THE CLEVERNESS OF THE CLEVER I WILL SET ASIDE."

Where is the wise man? Where is the scribe? Where is the debater of this age? Has not God made foolish the wisdom of the world?[5]

It is not surprising that some theologians call our age the most anti-intellectual period in the history of the church. This low view of reasoning and reflecting has led many outside the church to view Christians as shallow, simple and unintellectual. It has also made the church ineffective in reaching much of the world with the message of the gospel.

However, Scripture praises the use of our intellect. In Matthew 22:37 Jesus says that the greatest commandment is to love the Lord, not just with our heart and soul, but with our mind, or more literally, "understanding." There is no dichotomy between heart and head, reason and faith in Scripture. They work together, never apart. We cannot love God with just our heart—to love God requires us to understand him and the world he has made. Such understanding cannot be accomplished apart from employing the philosophical mindset.

"But then what role does faith play?" some ask. There is an important place for faith. Hebrews says that without faith it is impossible to please God (Heb 11:6). This not a blind faith, however; it is a reasonable faith. We believe God because we have good reasons to believe him; he has proven himself trustworthy. When God commanded Abraham to sacrifice Isaac, Abraham's faith was not a blind faith. He put his trust in God because God had proven himself to be faithful so many other times in the life of Abraham: in giving him a land, in providing a child through Sarah and in many other cases. Hebrews 11:17-19 tells us that Abraham remembered the promise from God that "in Isaac your descendants shall be called." So he knew that if God went through with the sacrifice, then

---

[5]This passage is not praising ignorance and condemning wisdom. Like the passage in Colossians, it is contrasting two kinds of wisdom: that of the world with that of the cross.

Isaac would be raised from the dead.[6] His faith was not blind faith. It was founded on the promise of a God who had proved himself trustworthy.

Acts 17 relates a story that occurred during Paul's second missionary journey. He and his companion Silas had crossed from Asia Minor into Macedonia. Having passed through Philippi, they arrived in Thessalonica. As was his custom, Paul went to the synagogue and reasoned with the Jews concerning the sufferings and resurrection of Jesus, concluding that he was the long-awaited Messiah. The reaction of the Thessalonian Jews was not favorable.[7] Stirred by jealousy, they gathered a mob to bring Paul and Silas before the people, releasing them only after a pledge was given that they would leave the city. Paul and Silas then moved on to the smaller and lesser-known town of Berea. Again Paul went to the synagogue to reason with the Jews, but here the response was much different: "Now these were more noble-minded than those in Thessalonica, for they received the word with great eagerness, examining the Scriptures daily to see whether these things were so" (Acts 17:11). It is important to note here that Luke praises these Bereans not just because they received the word with eagerness, but also because of the manner in which they received the word: "they examined the Scriptures daily to see if these things were so." These Berean Jews did not accept with blind faith what Paul taught. They subjected his claims to critical scrutiny because Paul claimed that Jesus fulfilled the requirements of what the Scriptures said Messiah would do. Imagine that. They were investigating Paul: the great apostle, the self-described "Hebrew of the Hebrews," a Pharisee trained under the greatest Pharisee of the day, Gamaliel. If anyone knew the Scriptures it was Paul. And yet these Bereans were making sure that Paul's teachings lined up with the evidence of the Scriptures. Luke calls them "noble-minded" for doing so. That is high praise for reasoning.

---

[6] The story in Genesis hints that Abraham was aware of this. When they arrive at the base of the mountain he tells his servants, "Stay here with the donkey while I and the boy go over there. We will worship and then we will come back to you" (Gen 22:5 NIV).

[7] Paul must have done more than just speak in the synagogue, as we are told that "many of them believed, along with a number of prominent Greek women and men" during his time there. These converts would become the foundation for the Thessalonian church that would sometime later be the recipients of the two letters to the Thessalonians found in our New Testament.

Luke is not the only biblical author to think highly of reasoning. Peter also exhorts us to apply our reasoning skills. In his first letter he exhorts the church to "sanctify Christ as Lord in your hearts, always being ready to make a defense to everyone who asks you to give an account for the hope that is in you, yet with gentleness and reverence" (1 Pet 3:15). Many may recognize this as the great apologetics verse (*apologia* means "defense"). Being prepared to defend our faith involves being able to reason with a certain degree of philosophical sophistication. Scripture counters the view of those Christians who devalue reason and intellectual rigor in the Christian life. The philosophical mindset is necessary to love the Lord and to be an effective disciple in these modern times.

A high view of the place of reason in the Christian life has been a cherished value throughout the history of the church. John Wesley offered this assessment of reason:

Suffer me now to add a few plain words, first to you who under-value reason. Never more declaim in that wild, loose, ranting manner, against this precious gift of God. Acknowledge "the candle of the Lord," which he hath fixed in our souls for excellent purposes. You see how many admirable ends it answers, were it only in the things of this life: Of what unspeakable use is even a moderate share of reason in all our worldly employments, from the lowest and meanest offices of life, through all the intermediate branches of business; till we ascend to those that are of the highest importance and the greatest difficulty! When therefore you despise or depreciate reason, you must not imagine you are doing God service: Least of all, are you promoting the cause of God when you are endeavouring to exclude reason out of religion.[8]

<hr />

[8]John Wesley, "Sermon LXX: The Case of Reason Considered," in *The Works of John Wesley*, 3rd ed., vol. 6 (Grand Rapids: Baker, 1986), pp. 359-60. John Calvin affirms much the same when he writes, "If we reflect that the Spirit of God is the only fountain of truth, we will be careful, as we would avoid offering insult to him, not to reject or condemn truth wherever it appears. In despising the gifts, we insult the Giver. How, then, can we deny that truth must have beamed on those ancient lawgivers who arranged civil order and discipline with so much equity? Shall we say that the philosophers, in their exquisite researches and skilful description of nature, were blind? Shall we deny the possession of intellect to those who drew up rules for discourse, and taught us to speak in accordance with reason? . . . shall we deem anything to be noble and praiseworthy, without tracing it to the hand of God?" (*Institutes on the Christian Religion*, trans. Henry Beveridge [Edinburgh: T & T Clark, 1863], II:2:15, pp. 245).

The second element in fulfilling Paul's mandate is the construction of a Christian worldview. According to Colossians 2:8, not only do we need to beware of deceptive philosophy, but also we need to establish a philosophy that "is according to Christ." We need to construct a Christian worldview. Since a primary source for that worldview is Scripture,[9] it is important that we handle Scripture correctly in establishing and constructing our Christian worldview.

Paul's second letter to Timothy is the most personal of all his epistles.[10] Most orthodox scholars agree that the epistle was Paul's last, written shortly before his execution in Rome in A.D. 68. Paul's purpose in the letter is to request that Timothy come to him in Rome and to offer final instructions and encouragement on the administration of the church. Several times he exhorts Timothy concerning the handling of Scripture. He affirms that "all Scripture is inspired by God and is profitable for teaching, for reproof, for correction, for training in righteousness" (2 Tim 3:16). He commands Timothy to pass the Word on to "faithful men who will be able to teach others also" (2 Tim 2:2). These men are to "preach the word" (2 Tim 4:2). As he did in Colossians, Paul presents a contrast in Timothy. This contrast is not between competing philosophies but between two kinds of teachers. In 2 Timothy 2:14 he describes those who "wrangle about words, which is useless and leads to the ruin of the hearers." Paul describes such teaching as "worldly and empty chatter" (2 Tim 2:16). He exhorts Timothy and the faithful men

[9]I want to emphasize that while Scripture is a primary source and the final authority for our Christian worldview, it is not the sole authority or the only source—a point that Calvin implies. God has provided a number of sources at our disposal to help us discover his truth. I will discuss this further below.

[10]I am aware of the debate concerning the Pauline authorship of the Pastoral Epistles. It is not within the scope of this book to enter into the details of this debate. The author holds the orthodox view of Pauline authorship and refers to the readers to discussions of this debate in other sources: Donald Guthrie, *The Pastoral Epistles: An Introduction and Commentary*, Tyndale New Testament Commentaries (Grand Rapids: Eerdmans, 1957), especially the appendix; Gordon D. Fee, *1 and 2 Timothy, Titus*, New International Biblical Commentary, ed. W. Ward Gasque (Peabody, MA: Hendrickson, 1988); I. Howard Marshall, *A Critical and Exegetical Commentary on the Pastoral Epistles*, International Critical Commentary (Edinburgh: T & T Clark, 1999); Ralph Earle, "1 Timothy," in *The Expositor's Bible Commentary*, ed. Frank E. Gaebelein, vol. 11 (Grand Rapids: Zondervan, 1978); and Ben Witherington III, *Letters and Homilies for Hellenized Christians: A Socio-Rhetorical Commentary on Titus, 1-2 Timothy and 1-3 John* (Downers Grove, IL: InterVarsity Press, 2006).

under his tutelage to "be diligent to present yourself approved to God as a workman who does not need to be ashamed, *accurately handling the word of truth*" (2 Tim 2:15, emphasis added).

The idea of diligence (*spoudason*) implies that this task will involve a certain degree of hard work, an idea reinforced by Paul's reference to Timothy being a "workman" (*ergatēs*), a term commonly used of a farmhand. The hard work involved in this case is "handling accurately the word of truth." The term for "handling accurately" is a translation of the Greek composite verb *orthotomounta* and is used only here in the New Testament. It literally means "to cut straight," and, like "farmhand," is used outside the New Testament to describe a plowman cutting a straight furrow—which is hard work indeed. Hence the KJV translates this phrase as "rightly dividing the word of truth." Ralph Earle states, "The context suggests that Paul is warning against taking the devious paths of deceiving interpretations in teaching the Scriptures."[11] Paul's contrast is between those who do not "handle accurately the word of truth" and those who do.

In order to construct a Christian worldview we need to "handle accurately the word of truth." There is a right way and wrong way to interpret God's Word, and we need to make sure we do it the right way. Unlike my friend Jeff.

I became a Christian while in college and got involved in a men's Bible study and discipleship group. One of the members of the group was Jeff, who became a good friend. One day Jeff announced to us all that he was going to become a vegetarian. When we asked why his reply was, "The Bible teaches that we should be vegetarians." We asked him where it teaches that, and his answer was succinct: "Daniel, chapter one."

In the Old Testament book of Daniel, the first chapter tells the story of Daniel and his three friends, Shadrach, Meshach and Abednego. They had been taken as prisoners into Babylon. The king of Babylon, Nebuchadnezzar, appointed a daily ration of food and wine for the Israelites, but Daniel refused to eat the food because it was defiled according to Jewish law. The commander of the officials, fearful that Daniel and his friends would look sickly when presented before the king and fearful

[11]Earle, "1 Timothy," p. 402.

that the king would blame him, pleaded with Daniel to eat the food prescribed for him. Instead Daniel offered a test: Let us eat vegetables and drink only water for ten days, and then compare us with others who had eaten the king's food and judge by what you observe. The result: "At the end of ten days their appearance seemed better and they were fatter than all the youths who had been eating the king's choice food" (Dan 1:15). The moral of the story: We should all be vegetarians. So said Jeff.

Well, no. While Jeff was zealous in his desire to follow Scripture, his enthusiasm might be a good example of zeal without knowledge (Rom 10:2). Few would agree that his interpretation and application of Daniel is on the mark. One principle of interpretation that Jeff was not considering has to do with passages in which the historical and theological conditions are different from what we find ourselves. This principle especially comes into play when we attempt to interpret and apply Old Testament passages. A frequent teaching found throughout the New Testament is that Christians are not under the same conditions or theological economy as the Old Testament Israelites, and many of their laws do not apply to Christians.[12] We cannot apply an Old Testament passage directly across time without taking into consideration its historical, literary and theological context. That was Jeff's mistake.[13] His hasty interpretation assumed there was no hermeneutical gap to jump.

Paul's exhortation to Timothy (and the church as a whole) is that we need to work hard to ensure that we interpret Scripture accurately. Interpretation is a philosophical enterprise. We establish principles of interpretation, like the historical-critical method, which is a philosophical principle, and then we employ the principle as we try to grasp the meaning of a passage.[14] Because Scripture is the primary (though not only) source for

---

[12]See Acts 15:6-21; Rom 6:14; Gal 2:15–3:14; Heb 7:18-19.

[13]One tool used in applying Old Testament passages is often referred to as the ladder of abstraction. The idea is to climb up the ladder and find a principle taught by that passage and then to climb back down to find a similar modern situation to which that principle might apply. In Dan 1 a principle that is clear is that we should be faithful to God and that he rewards such faithfulness. A modern similar situation might be the rampant sexual promiscuity in our culture and our faithfulness to God's teaching concerning sexual purity. We should trust that God will reward such faithfulness.

[14]We will discuss some of these principles further on. There are some who naively suggest that they do not interpret Scripture; they merely "read it as it is." I would suggest that every time one opens the Bible and reads from it with the intention of understanding it, that person is interpreting and hence is doing philosophy.

constructing a worldview that is "according to Christ," the need to interpret and apply it accurately is of extreme importance. We cannot perform this important task without employing the philosophical mindset.

The final element in fulfilling the biblical mandate expressed in Colossians 2:8 is refutation. Probably no other congregation of believers in the early church gave Paul more difficulty than did the church in Corinth. The city of Corinth was a port city in Greece and was famous for its debauchery and immorality.[15] It is believed that Paul established the church in Corinth around 50 to 52, during his second missionary Journey (Acts 18), and lived there for at least eighteen months. That the church was problematic is clear from both of Paul's letters to the Corinthians. In his first letter, Paul raises such issues as rivalry between parties, petty disputes between believers being brought to civil courts, incest in the church, disorderliness at the celebration of communion, an overall lack of love among the congregation and doubts about the resurrection. From the second letter we learn that Paul made a "painful visit" to Corinth between these two letters when he had to admonish them for deteriorating conditions within the body of believers. It is believed that he even composed a lost "severe letter" written "with many tears" (2 Cor 2:3-4) in which he again was forced to admonish them for problems.[16]

By the time Paul wrote his second letter to the Corinthians he was dealing with yet another problem that had arisen within that body of believers. This time the problem came from outside the church. A dissident group of Jews who claimed to be apostles had arrived in Corinth and were attacking Paul, claiming that he was a false apostle and that they were the true teachers of the gospel. Philip Edgcumbe Hughes writes, "This letter, accordingly, was written largely with the purpose of refuting the accusations and insinuations against him with which these intruders had been poisoning the minds

---

[15] In ancient times the city was so infamous that to refer to another as *Korinthiazomai* ("behaving like a Corinthian") was considered a grievous insult.

[16] The exact contents of this letter are unknown to us. Most scholars speculate from Paul's reference to the letter in 2 Corinthians that it was a personal, brief and severe letter. Some scholars suggest that 2 Cor 10–13 are this letter interpolated on the end of 2 Corinthians. For one refutation of this view, see Philip Edgcumbe Hughes, *The Second Epistle to the Corinthians: The English Text with Introduction, Exposition and Notes* (Grand Rapids: Eerdmans, 1962), pp. xix-xxxv.

of the believers at Corinth."[17] The bulk of Paul's defense of his apostleship begins in 2 Corinthians 10. He affirms that this war is not of the flesh but of the spirit (2 Cor 10:3-4). It is a war of ideas; these false apostles are teaching a different gospel, one that is contrary to Christ and is leading the Corinthian believers astray (2 Cor 11:3). Paul describes the task concerning such teachers in 2 Corinthians 10:5 (NIV): "We demolish arguments and every pretension that sets itself up against the knowledge of God, and we take captive every thought to make it obedient to Christ."

Notice how "thoughts" and "ideas" permeate Paul's defense here. Paul says his task is to demolish "arguments" (*logismous*, "calculated reasonings") and "pretensions" (*upsoma*, a term that refers to self-exalted, prideful thoughts) that are set against the "knowledge" of God and to take every "thought" (*nomeo*) captive to Christ. The parallel between this passage and Colossians 2:8 is striking. In that passage Paul contrasts vain and deceptive philosophy with that which is according to Christ. In this passage Paul contrasts arguments and pretensions set against knowledge of God with thoughts captive to Christ. The main difference between the passages is that in Colossians Paul exhorts readers to beware of those philosophies contrary to Christ, but in this passage Paul is more aggressive: we need to refute those contrary philosophies and demolish them.

Both passages make clear our task as Christian believers: in order to refute bad philosophy we need first to beware of it. Hence the need not just to develop a philosophical mindset but to study the writings of philosophers, to understand the different philosophical systems in order to discern those that are according to Christ as opposed to "arguments and pretensions" that are "according to the elementary principles of the world." Perhaps C. S. Lewis said this best:

To be ignorant and simple now—not to be able to meet the enemies on their own ground—would be to throw down our weapons, and to betray our uneducated brethren who have, under God, no defense but us against the intellectual attacks of the heathen. Good philosophy must exist, if for no other reason, because bad philosophy needs to be answered.[18]

[17] Ibid., p. xvi.
[18] C. S. Lewis, "Learning in War-Time," in *The Weight of Glory and Other Essays* (New York: Macmillan, 1980), p. 28.

Of course, not all are called to the vocation of professional philosopher. Lewis recognizes two categories of believers: the "uneducated brethren" and "us." There are those Christians who are uniquely gifted and called to perform the task of using philosophy to construct, explain and defend the Christian worldview and to educate other believers about that worldview. This is an important and noble task, and all are invited to consider this vocation. The fact that it is not for everybody as a vocation, however, should not be taken as an opportunity to neglect our duty to incorporate the philosophical mindset in examining and evaluating our own beliefs. Although we are not all called to philosophy as a vocation, we are all called to think critically.

Rather than repudiate the study and practice of philosophical reasoning, Scripture praises the use of our minds and our reasoning skills. It asserts that these skills are necessary to construct a Christian worldview and to refute those views that are contrary to Christ. A robust and vigorous philosophical mindset is necessary to fulfill the biblical mandate: to ensure that we are not kidnapped by hollow and deceptive philosophy but instead that we are able to construct, maintain and defend a philosophy based on Christ.

FUNCTIONS OF PHILOSOPHY FOR CHRISTIANS

I would like to suggest at least five ways philosophy plays a vital role for Christians. First, as we alluded to earlier, philosophy plays a large role in the task of hermeneutics, or interpreting Scripture. Every time we open the Bible and attempt to understand it, we are interpreting. Interpretation involves applying principles or criteria to discover the original meaning of the text. For example, one criterion is to interpret a passage according to its historical and literary context. This means we need to ascertain, as best as possible, the specific historical context of the passage we are reading. To whom was it originally written? What was the specific situation involved or the author's purpose in writing this passage? We also need to consider the literary context. What is going in the passages surrounding this one? How does this passage fit within the flow of the book as a whole? Now an important question is, Where do these criteria come from? They do not come from the Bible itself; nowhere in Scripture are we told how to interpret the Bible. These principles of interpretation are derived philosophically. Hermeneutics is a philosophical endeavor, and like most philosophical areas there is a wide range of perspectives on how interpretation should be done. I will discuss some of these principles further on.

Another aspect of hermeneutics is the task of application. The apostle Paul tells us, "All Scripture is inspired by God and profitable for teaching, for reproof, for correction, for training in righteousness; so that the man of God may be adequate, equipped for every good work" (2 Tim 3:16-17). However, while we can maintain the truth of this passage, we need only to be reminded of my friend Jeff to know that we need to be careful how we apply a biblical passage. At the minimum this means that we need first to apply the proper criteria in the interpretation of a passage. Then we must be careful that the manner in which we apply it is in accordance with those criteria. Such care involves employing the philosophical mindset.

A second role that philosophy plays for the Christian is in the task of doing theology. One famous ancient aphorism states: "Theology is the queen of the sciences, and philosophy is her handmaiden." Theology is a branch of study in which we organize our beliefs about God. A traditional way we do this is to systematize our beliefs into different subcategories: theology proper (the study of God), hamartiology (the study of sin), Christology (the study of Christ), pneumatology (the study of the Holy Spirit), eschatology (the study of end times). This is called systematic theology and necessarily involves philosophical thinking. Why? Because the Bible is not primarily a book of theology. The Bible is a collection of divinely inspired literature involving all sorts of genres: stories (both fictional and nonfictional), poetry, wisdom literature, letters, prophetic literature and others. If I were to ask you what the Bible teaches about the Holy Spirit, there is no one chapter called "Everything About the Holy Spirit" that you can go to. Systematic theologians sift through the entire text of Scripture, as well as what can be gathered from natural revelation,[19] and collect all the information about the Holy Spirit. However, their job is far from done. They need to organize this data, to work out apparent conflicts and to interpret what it all means. This involves the philosophical mindset. So while the Bible and natural revelation provide the raw data, philosophy provides the principles of systemizing that data into accessible categories where we can study and understand God and his creation.

Another way philosophy aids theology is in helping Christians to draw out and express important theological concepts. For example, a cardinal belief for Christians is the doctrine of the Trinity: God in three persons. It is often surprising to many Christians to find out that not only is the word *trinity* not located in the Bible, but there is not even a straightforward, clear statement of the doctrine.[20] This does not mean the doctrine is not in Scripture, for it can be inferred through bringing together a number of passages. However, the main problem is that the doctrine often appears as contradictory. How can Christians claim that there is only one God and yet affirm that the Father is God, the Son is God and the Holy Spirit is God? It sounds like we are claiming that there is one God and that there are three Gods at the same time, which clearly constitutes a contradiction.[21] The church fathers recognized this conundrum and appealed to philosophical concepts to express the Trinity: God is one *ousia* ("essence") eternally existing in three *hypostaseis* ("substances" or "persons").[22] Throughout the history of the church, Christian philosophers have often aided in expressing theological ideas such as the dual nature of Jesus and the issue of free will and divine sovereignty.[23]

---

[19]I believe that many evangelicals are ignorant of the important role that natural revelation plays in our understanding of theology. Although the Bible is the final authority in theological matters, it is not the only place where we learn important truths about God and his ways.

[20]Some Christians point to 1 Jn 5:7 (KJV) as a clear statement of the Trinity: "For there are three that bear record in heaven, the Father, the Word, and the Holy Ghost: and these three are one." However, the almost unanimous position of New Testament scholars across the theological spectrum is that this a later addition found only in some inferior manuscripts.

[21]As we will see, a primary principle in logic is that contradictions cannot be. See chapter five.

[22]It is outside the scope of the present discussion to elaborate on the complex historical development of the doctrine of the Trinity. The doctrine was eventually resolved at the Council of Constantinople (381) in which the Nicene Creed was affirmed.

[23]For recent examples, see Thomas Morris, *The Logic of God Incarnate* (Ithaca, NY: Cornell University Press, 1986), and Eleanor Stump and Norman Kretzman, "Eternity," *Journal of Philosophy* 78 (1981): 429-58.

A third area where philosophy functions for Christians is apologetics. Apologetics, from the Greek word *apologia* ("to defend"), is the rational defense of the truth claims of Christianity. From its earliest days Christianity has come under attack from those skeptical of its assertions. Questions have been raised about the existence of God, the apparent incongruity of a good God and the presence of evil, the possibility of miracles, the historicity of Jesus, and others. Apologetics is an attempt to address these questions by offering arguments and evidence to support Christian truth claims. Sometimes this is done by showing that a particular argument against Christianity is weak or does not follow. For example, David Hume argued that one should not believe a miracle claim because miracles are a "violation of the laws of nature," and the "firm and unalterable experience of mankind" has shown such laws cannot be violated. However, this is to assume that miracles have not happened in order to prove that they have not happened and is a classic example of the logical fallacy of begging the question.[24] Christian apologists also offer positive arguments to support their beliefs. For example, many Christian philosophers argue that moral values make sense ultimately only in a theistic world. If the universe and everything in it is merely the result of blind chance and material causes, from where does any ultimate value arise? Other Christian philosophers point to the incredible amount of intricate and complex detail in the running of the universe and argue that it is more probably the product of a highly intelligent mind rather than random chance. Probably in no other area of Christian thinking is the philosophical mindset employed than apologetics.

A fourth area where philosophy plays a part for Christians is polemics. If apologetics deals with external attacks against Christian beliefs, polemics deals with nonorthodox teachings that arise from within the church. Philosophy plays a role here in defending the doctrinal purity of orthodox Christianity. In the second half of the twentieth century, a number of Christian theologians were influenced by the ideas of Alfred North Whitehead. Whitehead, a philosopher, developed the idea that God is bipolar with two natures. One nature is transcendent and timeless while the other is integrally involved with the world, is part of the cosmic process itself and is always evolving. In fact God needs the world in order be a complete personal being. This came to be known as process theology. Some Christian theologians, such as John Cobb and Schubert Ogden, have suggested that this view of God is more in accord with the biblical view than the orthodox view of classical theism. To counter this idea, a number of Christian philosophers have defended the orthodox view of God and shown that process theology has a number of serious philosophical problems.[25] This is an excellent example of philosophy supporting the historical teachings of the church.

A final area where philosophy functions for the Christian is evangelism. As Christians we are all called to "go . . . and make disciples of all nations" (Mt 28:19). This commission requires that we interact often with those who differ from us in their basic worldviews and values. Being philosophically minded helps us to understand where others are coming from and to tailor our evangelistic message to meet their needs and questions. I will approach an atheist differently from someone of another religion (e.g., Judaism or Islam). For the atheist I might need to start with offering reasons to believe in God and the supernatural. However, a religious person would probably already believe in God and so she might just need to hear about Jesus. A nonbeliever who has been raised in the church his whole life would need to be approached differently. Although the gospel message is the same for all persons, the best way to effectively communicate that message differs depending on the specific needs of the individuals with whom we are sharing that message. Being an effective evangelist demands having an understanding of a person's worldview, and that involves a philosophical mindset.

The Role of the Bible in Doing Philosophy

For those Christians who take the Scriptures seriously, the question of their role in philosophical reasoning is of great significance.[26] I would

[25]See the collection of essays by Christian philosophers in *Process Theology*, ed. Ronald H. Nash (Grand Rapids: Baker, 1987) and the critique by Norman L. Geisler, "Process Theology," in *Tensions in Contemporary Theology*, ed. Stanley N. Gundry and Alan F. Johnson (Chicago: Moody Press, 1976).

[26]Christian attitudes and beliefs about the Bible vary widely from the conservative, holding to

like to suggest that there are two extremes that we should avoid concerning the role of the Bible in doing philosophy and then offer a middle way between these two extremes.

One extreme is to ignore the Bible while doing philosophy. There are some who argue that individuals should abandon their convictions, presuppositions and worldviews and adopt a position of neutrality in doing philosophy. They claim that philosophical investigation should be completely open to all views. Only after examining all possible views from a neutral perspective and submitting one's arguments to vigorous critical investigation should one then adopt the view that has the best evidence and arguments in favor for it. While this might seem appropriate and even responsible at first glance, there loom at least three problems with this concept of neutrality.

To start with, it is highly unlikely that most persons can do this. We have to have a starting point with which to begin in examining and evaluating beliefs and claims—some standard or criteria from which to examine and evaluate. Even the claim that we should be completely neutral is not above being examined and evaluated. Many of our foundational presuppositions—for example, that our senses are generally reliable, that other human beings have intelligent minds or that the laws of rational thought apply to reality—are almost universally acceptable criteria and yet involve some metaphysical commitments. Absolute neutrality seems to be an unrealistic and unattainable goal for the average person.

Second, even if complete neutrality were attainable, such a position seems unreasonable. For most of us, our presuppositions and worldview commitments are deeply ingrained. It seems unreasonable to require the average person of intelligence to rummage through his worldview introspectively and clear out all his foundational beliefs before he is even allowed to do philosophical inquiry. This would be a mammoth undertaking for even the most academically astute, much less the philosophical novice.

Finally, it is not necessary that a person abandon her worldview and

---

inspiration and inerrancy, to more liberal views for which the Scriptures play only a part in informing their faith. I am assuming that most who call themselves Christians take the Bible seriously at least in regards to its teachings on matters of faith, practice and ethics.

take a completely neutral position. We know from the general experience throughout the history of philosophy that great philosophical ideas and opinions have been expressed by those who have tenaciously clung to their worldview commitments, including those who have been Christians. It is true that critical investigation entails that a person should be as aware as she can be of her worldview and foundational beliefs and to submit those beliefs to critical examination. We have already discussed this in chapter one as the essence of philosophical speculation; such examination is at the heart of philosophy. Such examination, however, does not entail that a person abandon those beliefs prior to examining and evaluating them, and that includes beliefs founded on scriptural principles.

The other extreme was recently expressed by a student in one of my classes who asked, "Why do we need to study all of this philosophy? We have the Bible. It tells us everything we need to know. That's enough for me. I don't need to do philosophy." This idea, that the Bible is all we need and that all of our moral and metaphysical ideas must come from only that source, is a prevalent and, I believe, detrimental one among many Christians, especially those who aim to have a high regard for Scripture.

I believe the Scriptures are the inspired and inerrant Word of God and are the final authority on matters of faith, morality and knowledge of God's reality. My following comments should not be taken as impugning the Scriptures in any way. In fact, it is because of my high view of Scripture that I am so critical of this view. I think the Scriptures can and should be used by Christians in doing philosophy. But like anything that can be used, they can also be abused. I believe this idea, well-intentioned as it may be, ultimately misuses Scripture and borders on bibliolatry.

In a recent paper presented to members of the Evangelical Theological Society, J. P. Moreland addressed this problem, which he referred to as an overcommitment to the Bible. He stated:

The very idea that one could be overcommitted to the Bible may strike one as irreligious. In a sense this judgment is just. One could never be too committed to loving, obeying and promoting Scripture. In another sense, however, such overcommitment is ubiquitous and harmful. The sense I have in mind is the idea that that the Bible is the *sole* source of knowledge of God, morality and a host of related important items. . . . Clearly, the idea that from within the Christian point of view, Scripture is the *ultimate* authority, the *ultimate* source of relevant knowledge, does not entail that it is the *sole* authority or source. . . . Right reason, experience, creeds, traditions have all been recognized as subordinate sources of knowledge and authority within the Christian point of view subject to supreme and final authority of Scripture.[27]

Moreland's point is that there are many places where we can learn about God and his creation outside the Bible, a point that the Scriptures affirm:

The heavens are telling of the glory of God;
And their expanse is declaring the work of His hands.
Day to day pours forth speech,
And night to night reveals knowledge.
There is no speech, nor are there words;
Their voice is not heard.
Their line has gone out through all the earth,
And their utterances to the end of the world. (Ps 19:1-4)

The reasons why many Christians adopt this erroneous view of the use of Scripture are varied: a false dichotomy between faith and reason that has permeated modern thinking and marginalized religious truth claims to little more than subjective feelings; a problematic theological view of human depravity that denies the possibility of knowledge to nonbelievers; and a sincere but mistaken view that the Bible alone addresses every issue and need are a few examples. Whatever reason Christians have for adopting the idea, it has some severe problems and consequences, of which I will mention a few.

First, there are many important philosophical issues the Bible does not adequately address. This is not faulting the Scriptures, as they were not written to address every philosophical issue. For example, one branch of philosophy is epistemology, which has to do with knowledge

[27] J. P. Moreland, "How Evangelicals Became Overcommitted to the Bible and What Can Be Done About It," paper delivered to the 59th annual meeting of the Evangelical Theological Society, San Diego, CA, November 14-17, 2007.

claims. An important question in epistemology is, When can we say we know something? In other words, when does a belief become knowledge? This has to do with the problem of justification and is one of the current issues hotly debated in philosophy. The Scriptures do not address this important issue. Often when discussing justification in class a student will quote a passage from the Bible about knowledge: "The fear of the LORD is the beginning of knowledge" (Prov 1:7). One can affirm the veracity or value of this passage, but it does not answer the question of what knowledge is and when I know I have it. Many philosophical issues are not addressed in Scripture.

This leads to a second problem. Believers who adopt the attitude of "all I need is the Bible" often end up dreadfully misusing Scripture. The usual way this is done is through the highly mistaken but common custom of prooftexting. Believers often search anxiously to discover some verse or passage they presume will prove a particular point, all the while ignoring the serious exegetical work involved in interpreting and applying Scripture. Often they force a verse to say something it was never intended to mean and which usually has nothing to do with its original and historical and literary context. Rather than treating the Bible as a historical document written to the specific needs and issues of the original audience, and to be interpreted and applied appropriately, it is instead treated as a divinely authoritative version of Bartlett's book of quotations. This quote-a-verse mentality permeates the modern evangelical church and is problematic. An example might help illustrate the problem.

An important concept in ethics is the idea of the supererogatory act. These are moral actions an individual might perform that are right and praiseworthy but are not obligatory. In fact, they are often referred to as beyond the call of duty. Once, when discussing such actions, a student claimed that all right acts are obligatory and that he believed there are no supererogatory acts. He reasoned that one could never act beyond the call of duty, because if a right action can be done then one has a duty to do it. For his defense he quoted James 4:17, "Therefore, to one who knows the right thing to do and does not do it, to him it is sin." However, when studied in its context it becomes clear that this passage has nothing to do with the issue of supererogatory acts. It is condemning hypocrisy. James is addressing those who claim to be Christians but live lives that are contrary to that claim. He is not saying one is obligated do every right act that can possibly be done but that one cannot claim to be a Christian and then not do right acts. James's text was never meant to be applied in such an unlimited sense as this student was using it.

A third problem with claiming that the Bible is all one needs is that it is often ineffective in answering most philosophical questions for large numbers of people. Many people do not accept the Bible as the authoritative word on philosophical issues. Therefore, for these people, just because the Bible claims something, that does not in and of itself make it so. Just to quote a verse is not going to solve the problem or end the discussion for them. They desire to hear good reasoning and evidence. Quoting Scripture might convince those who already accept its authority, but that is a limited group of people. To those outside that group such an approach often comes across as shallow and simplistic—a reputation Christians desperately need to improve.

Finally, such a view fails to recognize that all truth is God's truth. God uses many avenues to communicate truths about his world. Reason, natural revelation and tradition are all venues through which God can and does reveal his truths to humankind. One has no reason to fear good reasoning and argumentation if they lead us to the truth, for they are then leading us to God, the ultimate source for all truth, beauty and goodness. At heart, philosophical inquiry and investigation is a search for truth and, for the believer, a search for God.

Does this mean we should never appeal to Scripture in doing philosophy? Certainly not. The Scriptures often can and should play a significant role in doing philosophy for the Christian. But it does mean that when we make such an appeal, we need to do so wisely, critically and strategically. That is the middle way between these two extremes. I suggest the following guidelines.

1. Do not feel obligated to appeal to a biblical passage in doing philosophy or to support a philosophical argument. You can often offer nonbiblical reasons and evidence for most philosophical positions. If these reasons are solid and true, then their value is equal to any biblical support you can offer because truth is truth. The advantage is that valid nonbiblical arguments gain wider appeal and acceptance as the reasoning is available for all to understand and follow and not just the limited group of those who accept Scripture as authoritative. Strategically, I suggest avoiding appeals to Scripture if they are not indispensable to an argument and if you are addressing those outside of the fellowship of believers.

2. Avoid prooftexting. If you do choose to appeal to Scripture in your philosophical work, then be sophisticated and accurate in your handling of it. This means you should avoid prooftexting a passage or verse. Here is a solid guideline: Never cite or quote a passage or verse without being aware of its literary and historical context. Return to the earlier discussions in this chapter on Colossians 2:8, 1 Timothy 2:15 and 2 Corinthians 10:5, and note how the historical and literary context of the passage is laid out and explained before discussing its application to the point being made. That is a good model to consider should you choose to use Scripture in your philosophical discussions. Once you are confident of the original context, strive to ensure that your interpretation and application line up with that context. This might mean that you will need to learn how to do the serious exegetical work required in handling Scripture.[28] Some might balk at the amount of work involved. But if you seriously believe you are dealing with God's word, then you should be willing to give it the time and effort demanded to be sure it is being handled correctly.

3. Be prepared to explain how the passage applies to the philosophical issue in accordance with its literary and historical context. If you choose to appeal to Scripture in doing philosophy, it is not enough to interpret it correctly. You need to show exactly how it applies to the particular philosophical issue under consideration. This is often the trickiest part of using Scripture. The danger of twisting a passage to communicate something it was never originally meant to convey is at its

---

[28]There are several excellent tools to help you, such as Bible commentaries, Bible dictionaries, atlases and language tools. There are also excellent books on Bible interpretation and study, such as William W. Kline, Craig L. Blomberg and Robert L. Hubbard Jr., *Introduction to Biblical Interpretation* (Nashville: Thomas Nelson, 2004), and Grant Osborne, *The Hermeneutical Spiral* (Downers Grove, IL: InterVarsity Press, 2006).

greatest at this point. You need to proceed with caution. There are many areas of philosophical discussion where Scripture is most relevant, in philosophy of religion for example, but there are other areas where you need to tread carefully and withhold strong conclusions. For example, it does seem that Scripture might imply some form of distinction between soul and body in the nature of humankind. In his discussion of life and death in 2 Corinthians 5, Paul seems to affirm the possibility of the person being "absent from the body" (2 Cor 5:6-8). However, you should be careful about extrapolating a full-blown Cartesian form of mind-body dualism from this reference, as some have done. The passage may lean in that direction, but it is not Paul's purpose to teach substance dualism here. Instead, he provides believers with hope in the face of death in trying times.[29]

4. Recognize the difference between the biblical text and your interpretation of the biblical text. Do not conflate the two. I commented earlier that every time we open the Bible and read it, we are interpreting. We cannot help doing it. Our own foundational beliefs about reality and our theological commitments influence the way we will often construe the meaning of a passage in Scripture. There is nothing wrong here as long as we are aware that there is a difference between the text and our interpretation of the text. The goal of good exegesis is to bring these two into line with each other. Sometimes this does not take much work, as the meaning may be apparent. Other times it may be a bit obscure, and we need to seriously study the context to determine the meaning of a particular passage. Often there are a number of possible meanings available to us, and we have to select the one we think is closest to the meaning the author meant to communicate, which leads to my next point.

5. Recognize the possibility of alternative reasonable interpretations of difficult passages. Some passages are difficult in determining exactly what an author meant. Either we do not have enough information or the context or wording is not clear. Often more than one meaning is possible. When that happens, we need to be open to other meanings and not take

[29]My point here is neither to affirm nor deny substance dualism, a view I hold, but to caution the use of this scriptural phrase as biblical proof for such a doctrine.

a dogmatic a stance on a particular reading of a passage. Epistemic humility is often a necessary virtue in scriptural interpretation. It is just as important to be confident of what you do not know as it is to be confident of what you do know. Two corollaries are implied here. First, we need to be charitable to those who take a meaning that might differ from our own. We can hold an opinion and yet disagree in a spirit of respectful dialogue with others whose opinions differ. Second, we should be open to changing our own interpretation of a passage if we believe the evidence requires it. Sometimes an adjustment is warranted, and any good philosopher needs to remain open to examining new information and arguments especially when it comes to these difficult passages.

6. Be aware of and take seriously the orthodox interpretations of the text as developed throughout the history of the church. For two thousand years intelligent people have been dealing with and interpreting the Scriptures. Throughout that time a consensus has evolved concerning the meaning of most of the text. The caution here is to take that tradition seriously as you approach your own study of the Scriptures. You should be suspicious of new and faddish interpretations. This is not to say that just because an interpretation is traditional it is automatically right. Sometimes evidence arises casting new light on the meaning of a passage that warrants a reconsideration of the traditional understanding of it. However, while you should not fall into the fallacy of thinking traditional means right, you should also honor long-held orthodox conclusions established by the historical church. We are not the first intelligent people to have opened the Scriptures, and we would be wise to consider the studies of those saints who have gone before us.

There is an important role for Scripture in doing philosophy. If you carefully and strategically follow the preceding guidelines, you can, at least at times, confidently appeal to the Scriptures to support philosophical arguments and conclusions.

CONCLUSION

In this chapter we have attempted to answer the question, What place does philosophy have for the Christian? We have looked at the biblical mandate for developing a philosophical mindset and saw that there are two philosophies available to us: one based on the "elementary principles of the world" and the other based on Christ and his teachings. We drew out three elements in fulfilling that mandate: the need to appreciate the value Scripture places on the use of our reason and intellect, the realization that philosophy is necessary to construct a Christian worldview and that philosophy is necessary to refute worldviews that are contrary to that of Christ. We then examined five ways philosophy plays a vital role in the Christian life and activity: hermeneutics, theology, apologetics, polemics and evangelism. Finally we discussed the important question of the role the Bible should play in doing philosophy. We rejected the extremes of not giving it any role on the one hand and using it exclusively on the other hand. I suggested an alternative between these two extremes through the critical and strategic use of Scripture. By critical I mean we use it in accordance to accepted standards of historical and literary interpretation and application. By strategic I mean that we appeal to it wisely, when necessary, and when specifically addressing believers. We should not feel pressured to feel we have to support every point with a scriptural passage, even if the Bible gives us excellent reasons to reject certain views, and we need to remember that all truth is God's truth.

four

THE DIVISIONS OF PHILOSOPHY

Perhaps you have heard the old riddle, "How do you eat an elephant?" The answer: "One bite at a time." The idea of eating an elephant, an enormous beast, would seem to most rather overwhelming. Yet if we were to reduce it to small bites, we could imagine that, given enough time and plenty of water, the task of eating one could be accomplished.[1] Like an elephant, philosophy is an enormous beast. It covers more than two thousand years of Western thought and encompasses questions on almost every imaginable subject.[2] It would be easy to get overwhelmed with the idea of mastering it. However, like eating an elephant, if we divide it into small bites, then, given enough time and plenty of water, we can begin to grasp it.

The study of philosophy can be reduced to smaller bites in a number of ways. One way is the historical approach. This method studies the development of philosophical ideas as they evolved over time by examining the works of the great philosophers and attempting to understand philosophical issues and questions within their historical context.

---

[1] I am not advocating eating elephants. Aside from ethical and health issues, I cannot imagine they are very tasty.

[2] I am intentionally discussing only Western philosophy. This is not to slight the importance of Eastern thought but to recognize the limits of this small book.

Western philosophy is usually divided into four historical periods.[3] Ancient philosophy (600 B.C.–A.D. 400) covers the beginning of Western philosophy, concentrating on the classical Greek and Roman philosophers. It is said that philosophy begins in wonder. These early thinkers looked out at the universe and pondered its origin and nature. Socrates, Plato and Aristotle came from this time. The medieval period (400–1400) was a time when the church was the dominant movement in the Western world. Often disparaged as the Dark Ages, this was a time of great philosophical output as Augustine, Thomas Aquinas, Anselm, Duns Scotus and William of Occam used philosophy as a way of expressing a Christian understanding of the world. The third historical period of Western philosophy began with the Renaissance, when there was a virtual explosion of knowledge, and continued into the modern period (1500–1900), when reason and science reigned as the supreme methods of discovery and knowledge. It was a colossal era of philosophical inquiry and includes the writings of many giants of the field: Bacon, Hobbes, Pascal, Descartes, Leibniz, Locke, Berkeley, Hume, Mill, Rousseau, Kant, Hegel, Schopenhauer and Kierkegaard, just to name a few. The fourth and current historical period is called contemporary philosophy. It began in the twentieth century and continues through the present day. Perhaps the most diverse age, it represents many different philosophical movements and perspectives with writers as varied as Husserl, James, Wittgenstein, Heidegger, Russell, Sartre, Camus, Kripke, Chomsky, Searle and Plantinga.

A second way to break the study of philosophy into smaller parts is the worldview approach, which examines philosophical problems and issues through the lens of different worldviews or whole systems of beliefs and then contrasts and compares the different systems with each other. You might remember that we defined a worldview in chapter one as a comprehensive system of beliefs that functions, first, as an explanation and interpretation of the world and, second, as an application of that system to the way people live and the values they hold.

There is no one definitive list of worldviews, and several catalogs

---

[3]Though the historical periods are somewhat arbitrary and debatable, most philosophers recognize the four periods outlined here.

have been suggested.[4] However, it can be safely said that all worldviews may be reducible to two primary ones, of which there are multiple variations: naturalism and nonnaturalism. Naturalism is the idea that all that exists are the constituents of the natural universe. That is all there is and all that can be known. The most common modern version of naturalism is scientific naturalism, which includes two basic aspects: (1) a naturalistic epistemic attitude that views scientific explanations as the only adequate means of explaining reality, and (2) a comprehensive story of reality that explains how all things came to be, told strictly in terms of event causation and described in terms of the laws of physics and evolutionary biology.[5]

Nonnaturalism is the view that there exists more than just the natural universe. Although there are nontheistic versions of nonnaturalism, such as Platonism, different forms of theism are the most common versions of nonnaturalism: monotheism, deism, polytheism, pantheism, panentheism. For example, Christian theism holds that there is a personal, all-good and perfect Creator who is omniscient, omnipotent and omnipresent. He is the source for all truth, value and beauty in the universe.

A third and perhaps the most customary manner of dividing philosophy into smaller parts is the topical approach. Philosophy is divided into branches of study with subcategories under the different branches. That is the approach I will take in this chapter. Below I first examine the three major branches of philosophy and some of the significant questions and problems under each branch and then briefly discuss some miscellaneous branches of philosophy.

THE THREE MAJOR BRANCHES OF PHILOSOPHY

To identify the major branches of philosophy, it would be helpful to recall the definition of philosophy from chapter one: Philosophy is the

---

[4]In *Understanding the Times*, 2nd ed. (Manitou Springs, CO: Summit Press, 2006), David Noebel lists Christianity, Islam, Marxism, New Age, postmodernism and secular humanism. James Sire lists eight worldviews: Christian theism, deism, naturalism, nihilism, existentialism, Eastern pantheistic monism, the New Age and postmodernism (*The Universe Next Door: A Basic Worldview Catalog*, 5th ed. [Downers Grove, IL: IVP Academic, 2009]).

[5]A more detailed description can be found in J. P. Moreland, *The Recalcitrant Imago Dei: Human Persons and the Failure of Naturalism* (London: SCM Press, 2009), pp. 5-6.

critical examination of our fundamental beliefs concerning the nature of reality, knowledge and truth, and our moral and social values. These three areas of examination form the three main branches of philosophy: reality, knowledge and values.[6]

Metaphysics. Metaphysics is the philosophical study of reality. The term is a combination of two Greek words, *meta* ("after" or "beyond") and *phusis* ("nature"). The story goes that when Andronicus of Rhodes was cataloging the works of Aristotle around 70 B.C. he encountered thirteen loose treatises following in sequence after Aristotle's *The Physics* and grouped these together and called them *Metaphysics* or "after physics." The term is apt not only for the sequencing of Aristotle's works but for their content as well. Aristotle referred to metaphysics as the "knowledge of immaterial being" and as "first philosophy." In other words, metaphysics is the study not only of the world we experience with our senses but also of those aspects of reality that are beyond the material world. As William Hasker states, metaphysics is more than just the study of reality, it is the study of what is *ultimately* real—what the basic constituents of all of reality are.[7] Metaphysics can be divided into four subcategories.

Cosmological metaphysics concerns questions about the origin and purpose of reality. Not to be confused with scientific cosmology, which limits itself to questions about the physical universe, metaphysical cosmology examines questions on the origin and purpose of ultimate reality. It is often said that the first philosophical question is, Why does anything exist at all? Everything we seem to encounter in the universe is contingent, which is to say nothing we observe seems to be necessary. Therefore, the obvious question becomes, If nothing needs to be here, then why is all of this stuff here? From this first question follows such questions as, Where did reality come from? When did it start? How did it develop into the way it is? What is the purpose of reality? Because time is an aspect of reality, was there a beginning to

---

[6]It should be noted that my purpose here is to survey the different branches of philosophy and introduce some of the common philosophical issues and questions under each of these branches. I am not covering all the varied answers offered to each problem.
[7]William Hasker, *Metaphysics: Constructing a World View* (Downers Grove, IL: InterVarsity Press, 1983), p. 14.

time? Does everything really exist contingently, or is there anything that exists necessarily?

Theistic metaphysics deals with questions about the reality of God. There are at least three general metaphysical questions about God that philosophers often ponder. First, is there a God, and what reasons do we have for believing in his existence? The statement "God exists" is more than just a faith claim. It is also a truth claim, which means reasons or evidence for its truthfulness should be examined. A number of arguments have been developed and debated in an attempt to answer the question of God's existence, such as the cosmological, teleological and moral arguments. A related question might be, Is there only one God? Monotheism has dominated Western culture, but other cultures have believed in polytheism, the idea that many gods exist.

A second metaphysical question concerns the nature of God. What is God like? Some Eastern philosophies say God is an impersonal force. Christian theism proposes that God is a personal being with a number of attributes: omniscience, omnipotence, omnibenevolence, infinity, eternality, immutability and a host of others. Philosophers attempt to reason about the meaning of these attributes and about possible inconsistencies in affirming them. For example, what does it mean to claim God is omnipotent? Does that mean he can literally do absolutely anything? As the old riddle says, can he make a stone so heavy that even he cannot lift it?

A third metaphysical question about God concerns his relationship to the rest of reality. Christian theism believes that God is intimately involved with his creation. He not only created all things but also sustains his creation and at times has intervened in it. Deism is the belief that, although God created the universe, he is not involved in it in any way. Deists deny the possibility of miracles, that the Bible is the Word of God or that Jesus Christ is God the Son, as these would entail God's intervention in the world. Pantheists believe that God and the world are the same thing: everything is God and God is everything. Panentheism is the bipolar view of God found in process theology. God is a part of the world and the world is a part of God. Philosophers also reason about the implication of each of these views. For example, if God created everything, as Christian theists claim, then what about evil? Did God create evil, and if he did not, then where did evil come from?

Our third subcategory of metaphysics, anthropological metaphysics, pertains to the nature of human beings. This topic offers a unique perspective in that humankind is both the subject as well as the object of its study. The overall question is, What does it mean to be a human being? All recognize that we have a physical body that operates according to the basic laws of physics and biochemistry. However, is there more to being human than just the physical? For the vast majority of human history most persons believed that we are more than just brains and bodies, that there is a nonphysical aspect of being human: the mind or soul. Many philosophers point to several recalcitrant facts of human experience such as consciousness and our ability to reason as evidence of a mind or soul beyond just the physical body. For many philosophers this traditional belief, called mind-body dualism, while common, carries with it a serious metaphysical problem. How can that which is in essence immaterial cause a physical event? Suppose I am sitting in class and I want to ask the teacher a question. I raise my hand, which involves a series of physical events—nerves travel down from my brain to my arm causing certain muscles to contract or expand, which causes my arm to rise. How can a nonphysical event, like the idea "I have a question," begin a causal chain of physical events that ends with my hand rising? For many philosophers this problem is so devastating that they abandon the idea of an immaterial soul or mind. For these materialists, we are just physical beings, and all mental events are either reducible or explainable in terms of physical events.[8] Dualists question whether such reductions are plausible. They wonder, "How do I explain consciousness only in terms of physical events?" This ongoing dialogue between dualists and materialists, the mind-body problem, is one of the most discussed and debated areas in modern metaphysics.

Another puzzling question concerning the nature of humanity refers to the idea of free will. Again, throughout history most people have naturally believed themselves able to make free choices and to act freely on those choices. In fact, we hold people responsible for the choices they make. The

[8]There are several varieties of both dualism and materialism. As this is a brief overview we will not discuss all the differing views.

idea of punishing people for crimes they have committed—at least in any punitive way—presumes that they were able to not commit them. Many philosophers, however, challenge the idea of libertarian free will. Some claim that our choices are ultimately determined by forces outside our control, such as our environment or our genetic makeup, and these directly determine our choices. Others, known as compatibilists, argue that we have free will, defined as doing what we want, but they claim what we want is based on beliefs and desires that ultimately are not in our control.

The fourth subcategory of metaphysics is both the most basic and the most abstract: ontological metaphysics.[9] Ontology deals with the nature of being or existence itself. Its primary question is, What does it mean for reality to exist? Ontology covers a broad group of questions concerning the nature of existence. One of the most primary concerns the problem of the one or the many: Is reality ultimately made of one thing and everything is just a part or expression of that one thing (monism), or is it made of up many things that exist independently of one another and cannot be reduced to one thing (pluralism)? In our discussion of the mind-body problem we encountered an example of these two views with physicalism (a form of monism) and dualism (a form of pluralism). Another ontological issue concerns the ideas of identity and change. What does it mean for something to be what it is? How does change affect identity? The ancient Greek philosopher Heraclitus commented that you cannot step into the same river twice because it is always changing. But if it is always changing, then is there ever a point in time when the river is ever actually there? What is the river itself? You have been changing your whole life both physically and psychologically, so in what sense are you the same person who existed five years ago, or even five minutes ago? Ontology also divides the basic constituents of reality into such categories as properties and substances, universals and particulars, and relations like causality and whole/part relations.

Epistemology. Epistemology is the branch of philosophy that deals with knowledge and truth claims. Aristotle said that all people by nature desire to know. However, we use the word *know* in at least three different

---

[9]Sometimes called general ontology.

ways. Sometimes we mean that we are acquainted with someone, as in "I know Frank" or "I know where the mall is." Sometimes we mean that we have acquired a skill: "I know how to play the trumpet." However, many times we claim to know certain facts: "Abraham Lincoln was the sixteenth president of the United States," "2+2=4," or "a carbon atom is composed of six electrons." It is this third type of knowledge, often called propositional knowledge, that is the main purview of epistemology.

The first task of epistemology is to define exactly what propositional knowledge is. In *Theatetus*, Plato defined knowledge as justified true belief. In order to claim that we know something we first have to believe it is true; second, it has to be true; third, we need good reasons to believe it is true. This is the tripartite definition of knowledge, and although it has been challenged and debated in recent years,[10] it is still generally considered the default starting place for a definition of knowledge. However, some philosophers, called skeptics, question whether we can have knowledge at all. There are different varieties of skeptics, but all of them doubt that at least some kinds of knowledge are possible.[11] A related question to skepticism is the question of certainty: Does one have to be certain before one can claim to know? Is certainty even possible?

For those who do believe we can have knowledge, the next question would be, How do we obtain knowledge? Empiricists claim that all knowledge begins with sense perception, the use of one of our five senses, so that if an idea cannot be ultimately traceable to an original sense perception, we cannot claim to know it. This raises further questions about perceptions: What does it mean to perceive something? Are my senses reliable in supplying information about the world? How do I know that? Can I arrive at *that* knowledge through my senses? The opposing view to empiricism is rationalism, which claims that knowledge begins in and is ultimately based on reason. Rationalists hold that I can arrive at some knowledge of the world through reason alone apart from

[10]Edmund Gettier developed a counterexample to this traditional definition that attempts to show one might have a justified true belief and yet would not consider it as knowledge. Philosophers have been debating the Gettier problem ever since.

[11]For example, global skeptics say we cannot know anything; local skeptics say we can have some knowledge about some areas but cannot have any knowledge about other areas.

the use of my five senses. For example, René Descartes believed that one could know that God exists by reasoning from the idea of perfection.[12]

If knowledge is justified true belief, what is truth? The nature of truth claims has been debated since the time of Jesus.[13] Some claim that truth is relative and there are no absolute truth claims.[14] However, most philosophers believe there are at least some propositions that we can claim are true. The question is, what makes a proposition true? Some believe that a proposition is true is if it corresponds with reality. If I claim "Carbon atoms have six electrons," that claim is true if in fact carbon atoms have six electrons. Others say that a proposition is true if it coheres with other propositions we know to be true. The above claim about carbon atoms would be true because it coheres with everything else we know about carbon atoms: their atomic mass and energy level and how they react with other elements. A third view says truth is what works in explaining a particular fact about the world or in accomplishing a goal. The claim about carbon atoms succeeds in explaining why carbon operates the way it does and therefore it must be true because it works. Each of these truth views has strengths and weaknesses.

Another important question in epistemology deals with the justification of our beliefs. For a belief to be justified means that we have reasons for holding that the belief is true. There are a couple of issues concerning contemporary epistemic justification. One has to do with our noetic structure, or the way our beliefs are related to one another. Most of our beliefs are related together in a chain. I believe *P* on the basis of *Q*, and I believe *Q* on the basis of *R*. One view of our noetic structure, called foundationalism, says that these beliefs build on one another and at the foundation of the structure are basic beliefs that are not built on other beliefs (see fig. 4.1).[15]

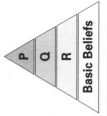

Figure 4.1.

---

[12]Immanuel Kant attempted to combine empiricism and rationalism. While my senses give me raw data, my innate reason provides the categories of understanding through which I interpret and comprehend that data.

[13]See John 18:38.

[14]They claim absolutely.

[15]What makes a belief "basic" varies according to which version of foundationalism one consid-

Some philosophers think there are fatal problems with foundationalism and so adopt a view called coherentism, in which no beliefs are more foundational than any other but instead relate together by cohering with one another. *P* is justified because it coheres with *R*, and *Q* is justified because it coheres with *R*, and *R* with *S* and so forth all around the web of beliefs (see fig. 4.2).

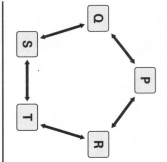

Figure 4.2.

A second debate in justification concerns ours epistemic duties. Many philosophers argue that if we are going to claim to know something, we have an epistemic obligation to have good reasons for our beliefs and that we should know what those reasons are. Because these reasons are internally accessible to us (we are aware of them inside our minds), this view is called internalism. Other philosophers think this requirement fails to account for at least some of our beliefs and is overly burdensome for making a knowledge claim. For example, I know what I had for breakfast this morning based on my memory of it. If asked how I know if my memory is true, I am warranted in holding that it is true even if I cannot give you a specific reason for believing that memories are generally reliable. As long as my memory apparatus is functioning properly, in the absence of a defeater,[16] I have no reason to doubt my memory of breakfast. These externalists[17] say that as long as our cognitive abilities are functioning properly, we are warranted or justified in claiming to know what we know. We do not even have to know they are functioning properly. In order to have knowledge, they just have to be functioning properly.

Axiology. The third major area of philosophical examination concerns

___

[16]A defeater is a proposition which, if true, would defeat a particular belief one might hold. So, If I were to hold a belief my friend was at the library this afternoon and somebody were to tell me that they saw him at the movies all afternoon, then that would be a defeater to my belief.

[17]They are called externalists because they look at our cognitive abilities from an external perspective as one would look at a machine functioning from the outside. There are a variety of

ers, but an example would be a self-evident truth like "the whole is greater than the part."

the idea of values. Almost everyone believes that at least some things in the world have value. We use value-laden language often to describe reality: "I read a *good* book last night," "It was *wrong* for Bill to cheat on his taxes," "You did an *excellent* job on that paper you wrote," "I think your reasoning is *terribly flawed*." These are evaluative claims and imply that we value or disvalue actions, results, events and a host of other kinds of things in the world. There are two major subdivisions to axiology.

Ethics deals with moral values: good versus evil or right versus wrong. Probably no other area in philosophy has occupied the thoughts of the average person more than ethics. We frequently ponder ethical questions on a personal level concerning our own character and actions as well as on a social level when we consider social issues such as capital punishment, war, abortion or euthanasia. Most of us adopt some position on these issues, and many of us have hotly debated these issues with family and friends, offering arguments in defense of our view. The fact that we have such debates shows something that we hold in common with our opponents: most of us believe that some actions are right and some actions are wrong. Nearly everyone would affirm that torturing little children for fun is morally wrong, and loving and caring for family is, at least *prima facie*, morally right.[18] However, some philosophers question the whole idea of morality. Some argue that morality is just an illusion and we have no moral obligations. Others argue that although there is something to morality, there are no objective or universal moral norms. Individual relativists, also called moral subjectivists, hold that morality is purely subjective and moral rules are relative to one's personal preferences or emotional state. Cultural relativists, also called conventionalists, argue that morality is relative to one's culture. Different culture groups have diverse moral norms. What may be right for one culture group at one time in history may be wrong for another culture group at another time in history. Since we are culturally determined, they argue that we have no real choice concerning our moral view—it is

---

[18]*Prima facie*, literally "at face value," means in normal situations without extenuating circumstances. One might be able to come up with a situation where caring for one's family is not an obligation (I have a hard time imagining what that might be) but apart from that the moral obligation to care for family is usually recognized as one of our deepest obligations.

dependent on the culture in which we were raised.

Throughout most of Western history most philosophers have believed that we do have at least some moral obligations and there are at least some actions that are right and some wrong. The question is how to determine what those are. A popular view is to appeal to the consequences of our actions: those actions that produce the best consequences are right and those that do not are wrong. The most common version of consequentialism is utilitarianism, which claims that an action is right if and only if it produces the greatest happiness for the greatest number of people.[19] If lying will produce more happiness than telling the truth, then I should lie. Other philosophers believe that consequences have nothing to do with an action being right. Deontologists argue that we have moral obligations regardless of consequences. Consequences are morally irrelevant. Moral duties are based on other factors such as divine commands, human nature, rationality or the inherent good of certain actions. So a deontologist might say that one should tell the truth even if the consequences are not good because there is value in truth-telling itself.

Recently some have revived an ancient view of ethics that concentrates not so much on what we do but on who we are. Virtue ethics claims that the debate about ethics has been misplaced and that our concern should be about developing our moral character. The thinking is that our actions typically stem from the kind of person we are, and so ethics should be mostly about training and inculcating moral virtues like faithfulness, integrity and charity. The person of integrity will keep commitments and deal with others justly because that is the kind of person he or she is.

We use the terms "good" and "bad" in another sense besides referring to moral values. If you stand outside your local movie theater as the patrons are exiting, you may hear them comment, "That was a good movie" or "What a stinker, I want my money back." When they use evaluative terms in this context they are not usually making a moral claim. They are speaking of a film's appeal and attraction. Christians believe that God has created human beings in a way that we are attracted to the

---

[19]There are several different forms of utilitarianism that replace the value "happiness" with some other value.

beautiful and pleasing. The field of philosophy that raises questions about art and beauty is aesthetics. Since an aesthetic claim is a value judgment, it is considered a subcategory of axiology.

The first question in aesthetics is, What is art? The word *art* is short for "artifact," which describes any human-made object.[20] However, when we use the word *art* we usually mean more than a human-made object. Garbage is made by people, yet few would consider it art.[21] Defining art is not easy. Some have suggested that art is whatever is presented as art or designated as art by an artist. A related definition is that art is the product of the artistic process. Many of these have characteristics we recognize as pertinent to art: skill, complexity, design, intelligence. However, many of us have seen works presented or designated as art that we have seriously questioned should qualify as works of art. For example, Marcel Duchamp is a representative of the school of art known as Dadaism, an antirational art movement. One of Duchamp's most well-known works is the *Fountain*, which is a urinal lying on its back with the words "R. Mutt" written on the side. The response of many observers is, "Interesting, but is it art?" The definition of art is elusive.

Another important question is the function of art: What is its purpose? Some believe that the purpose of art is imitation. For many the best works of art are those that come closest to imitating an aspect of reality such as an event, person or object. In Beethoven's great choral masterpiece, *Missa Solemnis*, one aurally experiences the crucifixion, burial and resurrection of Jesus through the way the text is painted in the instrumentation of the orchestra. Others hold that the function of art is not so much imitation as the expression of emotions or ideas. A great poem or symphony will emotionally move us into the pits of despair or to the heights of heaven. Or a play like Arthur Miller's *Death of a Salesman* might cause us to question the tyranny of relentlessly chasing the American dream. Some say that the purpose of art is to perfectly express a particular form, such as the sonata-allegro form found in

---

[20]As a field aesthetics is usually restricted to human-made artistic endeavors. This is not to deny there is great natural beauty in the world that arouses our aesthetic sensibilities. Much can be said about this natural beauty, but for our purposes we will primarily restrict our discussion to human-made art.

[21]Though it is possible to create art out of garbage.

Haydn's symphonies, while others disagree and say that it is the purpose of art to break forms and exist always on the cutting edge. Hence John Cage breaks all musical forms in his work titled "4'33", a work in three movements that is silent—there is no music at all.

One of the reasons art is difficult to define or determine is due to the modern propensity to view beauty individually and subjectively. However, this raises one of the most perplexing questions about art: Is beauty truly just in the eye of the beholder, so that there are no objective standards to art, or do objective standards exist to help determine art from nonart or good art from bad art? Aesthetic subjectivism holds that beauty is not in the object itself but in the person who is interacting with the object. Hence, whether an object is beautiful changes from person to person. This view is popular, but it usually does not stand up well under close inspection. The fact that we even have art museums or the Academy Awards demonstrates that we recognize the difference between a kindergartner's finger painting and Salvador Dali's *The Last Supper*, or between Steven Spielberg's *Schindler's List* and Ed Wood's *Plan 9 from Outer Space*. It seems that most of us hold to some form of aesthetic objectivism. While there would be some debate over what constitutes objective standards for art, most would agree that at a minimum art should exhibit a high level of skill, diligence, complexity, design and intelligence.

Miscellaneous Branches of Philosophy

Most questions in philosophy can be subsumed under one of the three major branches, but a number of traditional divisions of philosophy stand alone and are worth mentioning.

Political philosophy is sometimes called ethics for society and is often thought of as another subbranch of axiology. Politics broadly conceived refers to how people within a society relate and function together. Political philosophy addresses a number of questions. What is the best way to govern a people? Monarchy, oligarchy or democracy? Should authority reside in the hands of one person, like a monarch or a dictator, or in the hands of all persons equally, as in a pure democracy, or should it be in the hands of representatives, as in a republic? A major area of concern for political philosophy is justice. What method of distributing goods and services in society is most just? In the United States we promote the free market exchange of capitalism where goods and services are distributed based on one's ability to pay. Some suggest that capitalism is not fair to those who are poor (who cannot pay) and that a communistic system that distributes goods and services equally to all regardless of ability to pay is more just. How do we best balance individual rights and liberties with the needs of society? The rise of terrorism in the West has resulted in many arguing that we need more invasive security procedures such as wiretaps and full-body scans at public venues like airports. Others decry this as unwarranted invasion of privacy. When do the needs of society warrant the infringement of private individual rights?

Philosophy of religion deals with questions concerning the nature of God and how we know and relate to him. Under philosophy of religion we move beyond just the questions of God's existence and more into questions of his nature, attributes and actions. For example, is God a personal being or an impersonal force? Does he exist independently of the rest of reality, or is he a part of everything? Is he involved with creation, as theism holds, or does he stand back from it, as deism claims? What does it mean to say that God is omnipotent? Does that imply he can do absolutely anything? Are miracles possible, and how can we identify one as coming from God?

Philosophy of religion also deals with questions of how we relate to and know about God. What is the relationship between reason and faith? How should we evaluate claims of religious or mystical experiences? Philosophy of religion deals with those areas where belief in God might conflict with other beliefs. When it appears that science is telling me one thing about reality but religious sources, like Scripture, seem to say something completely different, how do I resolve the conflict? Finally, one of the most difficult conflicts concerns the problem of evil. Some argue that if God is all-good, then he would want to rid the world of evil, and if he is all-powerful, he can rid the world of evil. So, why does evil exist? How do we reconcile these two?

Philosophy of history can be thought of in two senses. First there is the inquiry into the nature of history itself: Does it have a purpose? Is it linear or circular? What is the significance of history? This is usually called speculative philosophy of history and is closely related to metaphysics, as it deals with the ontology of history. The other sense of philosophy of history concerns the inquiry into how history is known. Here one is dealing with the task of historians in determining what has happened in the past and its meaning and importance for us today. This area is often called critical philosophy of history or historiography. It is closely related to epistemology, as it deals with how we know history. What exactly does the historian study? Our immediate reply might be "facts of the past." However, this immediately raises several questions. What constitutes a fact? And if the fact is something that happened in the past, then how can we presently study it? It becomes clear that history is not the study of past facts but the study of the record of those past facts, primarily written sources. However, this raises even more philosophical questions: What are the criteria for determining the reliability of sources? Because history is written by persons who are culturally and historically conditioned, how much subjective bias and individual coloring influence historical records? How much will a history of the American Civil War differ if written by a southerner rather than a northerner? Is historical objectivity even possible? Also, history is not simply the study of facts of the past. Most everyone knows that Lincoln delivered the Gettysburg address, but few know or care what he had for breakfast that morning. History is the study of significant facts of the past. This raises even more philosophical questions: What makes a fact significant, and who makes those decisions?

Philosophy of law is more commonly known by the term *jurisprudence*, meaning the study and theory of law. Issues in the area of jurisprudence range from the nature of law to the relationship between law and morality. Jurisprudence differs from the related field of legal ethics in that issues of legal philosophy are more wide-ranging than issues of legal ethics. For instance, the question of whether the death penalty is morally just would be considered a matter of legal ethics, whereas the question of whether courts are justified in imposing punishment falls under legal philosophy. Philosophers of law seek to answer certain questions. What is law? What is the intention of law? How does law relate to morality?

One classic debate in jurisprudence involves the sources of law. The positivist view argues that there is no connection between law and morality and the only sources of law are those that have been expressly enacted by a government or court. The naturalist view takes the position that government is not the only source of law, but moral values, human nature and God-given rights are also integrated in the law. Under natural law, something should be illegal because it is wrong. In contrast, positivism holds that something is wrong because it is illegal. How would a positivist justify the laws of Nazi Germany, which are generally considered abhorrent to natural law? However, how would one naturalist claim that abortion is wrong while another naturalist may assert the opposite? Because natural law is assumed and not based on established rules, it is subject to greater interpretation. Legal philosophers strive to analyze these different theories in order to have a greater understanding of jurisprudence.[22]

Another area closely related to epistemology is philosophy of science. For many modern thinkers, science is the primary means of understanding and explaining the observable natural world around us. In fact, some claim that science is the antithesis of philosophy. After all, they reason, science is about cold hard facts and philosophy is little more than speculation and subjective opinion. Such claims are a bit naive and simplistic about both science and philosophy. Even defining science and delineating its boundaries and limitations requires a fairly sophisticated philosophical analysis. There is no "scientific" definition of science. And many definitions of science that have been supplied by scientists have been shown to be inadequate. For example, the description of science above mentions the observable world, which is a standard idea in a typical definition of science, as most scientists insist that they deal only with empirical facts. However, scientists often infer conclusions about unobserved causes based on observable effects: the magnetic field, the subatomic world and black holes. So if observable means direct observation, then science is not always dealing with the observable.

One of the most important debates in philosophy of science has to do with what science is supposed to be telling us. One view, called scientific realism, claims that the purpose of science is to give us a truthful expla-

---

[22]I am indebted to Lindsay C. Leonard, Esq., for her contribution on this discussion of philosophy of law.

nation and understanding of the world. So a scientific theory is attempting to explain what is really happening in the theory-independent world. When a realist speaks of electrons, he is talking about actual entities that exist inside atoms. This is the way most individuals think of scientific theories. However, many scientists today have abandoned the search for truth and have adopted a view called scientific antirealism. Antirealists claim that the purpose of scientific theories is not to tell us the truth about the world but to do something else. There are different versions of antirealism, but the most common version is instrumentalism.[23] Instrumentalism claims that the purpose of scientific theories is to function as a way of explaining, predicting or understanding certain observable phenomena. It adopts the pragmatic view of truth—what is true is what works to explain something. So when the antirealist talks of electrons, he is not saying these things actually exist (though they might), but that they are useful fictional concepts that explain operations in the subatomic world. It is just this issue of truthfulness that makes some realists uncomfortable with an antirealist approach. However, the two views are not necessarily mutually incompatible, and it may be that in some cases a realist approach is warranted and in others an antirealist approach may be the best way to explain a scientific theory.

This brief overview of miscellaneous branches of philosophy demonstrates an important element of philosophical speculation. Every area of study and activity involves basic foundational features that are philosophical in nature. That is why the highest degree one usually obtains in a given field is the doctor of philosophy. The definition and nature of a field is, fundamentally, a philosophical matter. So whether we are taking about sports, literature or motion pictures, if taken to the ultimate foundational level of what it is and why it is, one will be discussing the philosophy of _____. You cannot get away from philosophy. Everything bottoms out here.

[23]There are also several different versions of antirealism, such as phenomenalism, operationalism, pragmatism and constructive empiricism. See J. P. Moreland and William Lane Craig, *Philosophical Foundations for a Christian Worldview* (Downers Grove, IL: InterVarsity Press, 2003), pp. 335-40 for a discussion of these versions.

five

A LITTLE LOGIC

I have always been somewhat envious of auto mechanics. Like many newly married couples, my wife and I struggled financially in the early years of our marriage. Our first cars were clunkers and needed constant maintenance. We could never afford to take them to a skilled mechanic. Many Saturday afternoons you would find me lying in the driveway underneath one of our cars changing the oil or attempting to put in a new set of brakes. I envied those auto mechanics for their skills and for their garages with hydraulic lifts. But mostly I envied them for their tools. You can understand what I mean if you have ever tried to work on a car with just a screwdriver and pair of pliers. How often I wished for a first-class ratchet set along with an air-powered driver. With the right tools even the most difficult job can be performed with relative ease. In the hands of a skilled mechanic, the right tools can produce a work of art.

Every field employs certain tools to accomplish the necessary tasks in that field. The skillful use of these tools will often determine one's effectiveness in operating in that field. Auto mechanics use wrenches and ratchets. Surgeons use scalpels and souchers. Carpenters use hammers and saws. Philosophers use logic. The first task in being an effective philosopher, then, is to learn how to use the tools of philosophy, and that means becoming a skillful logician. Therefore, the second half of this book will introduce you to logic and argumentation. We begin with a discussion of the foundation for logical reasoning.

THE LAWS OF LOGIC

At the foundation for all reasoning are the laws of logic, often referred to as the first principles of logic.[1] The laws of logic make discourse possible. If they are not recognized as true, then nothing we claim makes any sense. Therefore, it is important to have a firm grasp of these laws.

There are traditionally three laws of logic. The first and perhaps most primary law is the law of noncontradiction, which states: Something cannot both be and not be at the same time and in the same respect. The law of noncontradiction can be expressed symbolically: $\sim (P \bullet \sim P)$.[2] The $\sim$ means "not" or "non" and negates any term or proposition that follows it. The parenthesis means "both." The $\bullet$ means "and." The letter P is called a variable, and it can refer to any term or proposition. Therefore the logical formula reads, "It is not the case that there can be both P and non-P." Stating it this way clears up some confusion concerning the law of noncontradiction. A student once asked, "But it seems to be saying that everything is either black or white. Aren't things sometimes gray?"[3] The formula clears up this confusion. The logical opposite of black is not white but is nonblack, which would include any color, including gray.

There is never an exception to this law. The medieval philosopher Avicenna, tired of the intellectual games of sophists, wrote, "Anyone who denies the law of non-contradiction should be beaten and burned until he admits that to be beaten is not the same as not to be beaten, and to be burned is not the same as not to be burned."[3] Contradictions cannot be. In spite of the foundational aspect of this law, I often encounter persons who think they can prove contradictions are possible. A student once stood up in class and walked over to the open door of the room. He stood on the threshold, placed one foot in the classroom and one in the hallway and claimed that he was both inside the room and outside the room at the same time. Hence the law was not true—or so

---

[1] In philosophy a first principle is a basic, foundational proposition or group of propositions that cannot be deduced from any other proposition. First principles are self-evident truths that form the starting point for a particular branch of philosophy.

[2] For precision and accuracy, logicians often express these laws by employing symbols in logical formulas similar to scientific or mathematical formulas.

[3] Avicenna, *Metaphysics*, 1, commenting on Aristotle, *Topics* 1.11.105a4-5. Sophists were enamored with persuasive speech but contributed little in the way of substance.

he claimed. However, this student was neglecting an important element of the law: Something cannot both be and not be at the same time and in the same respect. He had placed part of his body in the room and part out of the room at the same time. I challenged him to place his entire body both inside the room and outside the room at the same time. He quietly slunk back into his seat.

Some Christians have challenged this law by claiming that God is omnipotent (all-powerful) and therefore can do anything, including contradictions. They will often quote Matthew 19:26, where Jesus says, "With people this is impossible, but with God all things are possible," as proof of their claim. There are a couple of problems with this reasoning. First, the context of this passage is salvation. Jesus is speaking of how difficult it is for a rich person to be saved because he often clings to his riches instead of trusting God. Jesus uses two hyperboles to make his point. The first is that of a camel going through the eye of a needle, and the second is "with God all things are possible." These are both hyperbolic statements.[4] He no more means "all things" to be taken absolutely and universally than he does a real camel going through an eye of a needle. His point is that none of us can save ourselves; only God can save us. Second, when he says "all things are possible with God" he means "all things that can possibly be are possible with God." There are some things that cannot possibly be: contradictions. For example, God cannot both exist and not exist at the same time and in the same respect. He cannot be God and also not be God. That is a contradiction, and contradictions are impossible.

This has nothing to do with omnipotence. There are some things that, by their nature, are not possible. A triangle with only two angles cannot be because it would no longer be a tri-angle. A married bachelor is impossible because he would be a married-unmarried person, and that makes no sense. Even God cannot create such things, not because he does not have the power but because such things cannot be.[5]

---

[4] A hyperbole is an exaggeration employed to enhance the point the speaker is making. It is a legitimate rhetorical device employed to leave a strong impression but not to be taken literally.

[5] Some Christians become alarmed with the claim that there are things God cannot do. However, even Scripture affirms this truth. For example, Titus 1:2 tells us God cannot lie. Further, a cardinal Christian doctrine affirms that God cannot sin.

The second law of logic is the law of excluded middle, which states: Something either is or is not, or P v ~P. The v in this formula, called a wedge, means "either/or." So the formula reads, "Either P or non-P." It is called the law of excluded middle because it excludes the possibility of something in the middle of existence and nonexistence. A thing either exists or it does not; there is no *tertian quid* ("third what"). There is no such thing as something half-existing and half not-existing because the part that is half not-existing would have to exist as a nonexisting part of the thing, and that makes no sense.

The third law of logic is called the law of identity, which states: Something is what it is. Stated as a formula, it reads, "P = P." This may be the most obvious law, as it claims that whatever a particular thing is, it is that particular thing. The law takes into account that different terms might refer to the same thing. For example, "Clark Kent" and "Superman" are two different terms, but they refer to the same individual.

A few comments need to be made about these three laws. First, the observation has been made that these three laws all seem to be saying the same thing. In a sense that is true. They mutually entail each other to the point where if one is true, then the others follow. However, they are distinct in that they each emphasize a different logical relationship, and in logical discourse, one law may be more useful than the other. Noncontradiction seems to have the primary force in most logical reasoning. However, excluded middle often is the best way to express a point in an argument.

Second, as stated above, these laws are claims about existence. However, they can also be stated as claims about the truthfulness of a proposition. The law of noncontradiction can be stated: A proposition cannot be both true and false at the same time and in the same respect. The law of excluded middle can be stated: A proposition is either true or false. These both mean that no propositions are both true and false; they are either one or the other.[6] If a person claims, "Last night I went to the store and bought ice cream," and it turns out he went to the store but did not buy ice cream, then the proposition is false, not partly false and

---

[6]Many philosophers follow Aristotle and hold that some propositions about the future are neither true nor false.

partly true. The third law can be stated: All true propositions are true, and all false propositions are false.

Finally, these laws are not in need of any proof beyond themselves. They are self-evident and undeniable. By self-evident it is meant they prove themselves and do not need any proof outside themselves. Undeniable mean that the laws cannot be meaningfully denied. Any person denying these laws has to use them as the basis for the denial. Hence a denial would be self-defeating: she would be defeating the very point she is trying to make.

The Language of Logic

If philosophy is thinking critically about our beliefs, then logic can be seen as critically thinking about how we critically think. However, the word *think* may be too broad for our purposes. "Thinking" describes any mental activity, including remembering, daydreaming, supposing, believing, wishing and reasoning. Logic mostly concerns itself with the last of these. *Reasoning* is at the heart of what goes on in the process we have been describing as critical thinking. Logic employs established rules for correct reasoning, which we then use in evaluating our own reasons for the beliefs we hold.

When we group our reasons together to achieve a particular conclusion, we refer to that as an *argument*. An argument is a group of propositions,[7] some of which are reasons (called *premises*) trying to prove one of the other propositions (called the *conclusion*). Notice the simple argument below:

(a) All men are mortal.
     Socrates was a man.
     Therefore, Socrates was mortal.

The first two propositions are the premises and the last is the conclusion. In addition to the premises and the conclusion there is a third element to an argument: the *inference*. The inference is the relationship between the premises and the conclusion. We use metaphors to de-

---

[7] A proposition is a statement that affirms or denies something and has truth value. While all propositions are sentences, not all sentences are propositions. Questions, commands and exclamations do not express propositions.

scribe this relationship. We will say either that the premises *lead to* the conclusion or that the conclusion *follows from* the premises. Note the following argument:

(b) John Adams was the second president of the United States.
The square root of 81 is 9.
Therefore, I love pizza.

In this argument we have two premises and a conclusion, but there is no inference between them. An argument put forth in which there is no inference is called a *non sequitur*, which means "it does not follow."

Logic is about evaluating arguments. Deductive arguments are evaluated as either *valid* or *invalid*. Inductive arguments are either *strong* or *weak*. If the conclusion follows from the premises, then it is either valid (if deductive) or strong (if inductive). Our first argument above is a valid deductive argument and the second is not. When it comes to the propositions within the argument we evaluate them according to their *truth value*: whether they are true or false.

The validity or strength of an argument and the truth value of the propositions are two distinct and separate aspects of an argument. *The truth value of the propositions in an argument has nothing to do with its validity or strength, and validity or strength has nothing to do with truth value.* An argument can be valid or strong with all false propositions, and it can be invalid or weak with all true propositions. Look at the two deductive arguments below:

(c) All cows are purple animals.
All purple animals jump over the moon.
Therefore, all cows jump over the moon.

(d) All U.S. presidents have been male.
Abraham Lincoln was male.
Therefore, Abraham Lincoln was a U.S. president.

In argument (c) all of the propositions are false, yet the conclusion is valid. This is because the conclusion follows from the premises whether they are true or not. In a valid deductive argument, *if* the premises are assumed to be true, then the conclusion follows. *If* all cows are purple and *if* all purple animals jump over the moon, then it would have to be the case that all cows jump over the moon. When we evaluate the validity of an argument, we are not concerned with whether the premises are true or not. We will discuss this more when we discuss deductive and inductive arguments below.

Notice in argument (*d*) that all of the propositions are true, yet the argument is invalid. This is because the conclusion does not follow. The fact that all presidents have been male and that Lincoln was male does not lead to any conclusion. It happens to be true that Lincoln was president, but that does not follow from these two premises. You can easily test the validity of this argument by substituting the name of any male person in the second premise and will see immediately that the conclusion does not follow. This discussion brings out an important point: Do not assume that because you agree with the conclusion of an argument it must be a good argument. I have often heard arguments where I agree with the conclusion but thought the argument itself was poor. Be careful about proclaiming that an argument is valid or strong simply because you like its conclusion.

A final term we need to introduce is *soundness* (for deduction) or *cogency* (for induction). A deductive argument is considered sound when it is valid and the premises are true. An inductive argument is considered cogent when it is strong and the premises are true. Argument (*c*) is valid but unsound because the premises are false. In order to be sound, a deductive argument must be both valid and feature all true premises. It is unsound if either the argument is invalid, at least one premise is false, or both. Only one of the above arguments is sound. Can you determine which?[8]

DEDUCTION

Deduction is a form of logical reasoning in which the aim is to arrive at a conclusion that is logically necessary given the premises. In a valid deductive argument, if the premises are assumed to be true, it is impossible for the conclusion to be false. It is important to note that this definition is not claiming that the premises are true. It claims that, if one *assumes* the premises are true, then the conclusion must be true if the

---

[8]The correct answer is (*a*).

reasoning is valid. In a valid deductive argument, the premises guarantee the conclusion with logical certainty.

The arguments we employed above previously were all deductive arguments, though they were not all valid. Assuming the premises are true, the conclusion follows necessarily. If it is true that all men are mortal and that Socrates was a man, then it must be true that Socrates was mortal. It is impossible for the conclusion to be false if the two premises are true. Argument (a) was a valid deductive argument. Assuming the premises are true, the conclusion follows necessarily. If it is true that all men are mortal and that Socrates was a man, then it must be true that Socrates was mortal. It is impossible for the conclusion to be false if the two premises are true. Argument (c) was also valid. In that argument the premises are not really true. However, *assuming* they are true, it is impossible for the conclusion to be false. It follows necessarily from the two premises: *If* it is true that all cows are purple and *if* all purple animals jump over the moon, then it *must* be true that all cows jump over the moon.

The key distinctive of a deductive argument is the kind of conclusion that one is aiming to obtain: one that *must* follow given the premises. It is often claimed that a distinctive feature of deductive arguments is that they argue from the general to the particular. Although this is common, it is not the key distinguishing feature and is not always the case. Argument (a) follows this pattern but argument (c) does not. The key distinctive has to do with the kind of conclusion entailed. We will contrast this with induction below.

There are many different forms of deductive arguments. An argument based on mathematics is a deductive form of reasoning: $265 + 573 = 838$. The conclusion, 838, follows necessarily from the premises added together. The most common form of deductive reasoning is the *syllogism*. A syllogism is a logical argument that consists of two premises and a conclusion that is structured according to certain *rules of valid inference* that govern the particular type of syllogism being employed. If the syllogism keeps the rules, it is valid. If it breaks any of them, it is invalid. There are three different kinds of syllogisms that are based on three different kinds of propositions used in reasoning.

The first of these is the *categorical syllogism*. A categorical syllogism consists of two categorical propositions as the premises and one categorical proposition as the conclusion. A *categorical proposition* is a statement that affirms or denies a relationship between two categories or classes: a subject and a predicate. The claim of a categorical proposition is that one of these categories is included or not included as a member of the other category. Here is an example: "All students are kind." In this proposition it is being affirmed that all the members of the subject (students) are also members of the predicate (kind persons). As table 5.1 shows, there are four and only four kinds of categorical propositions.[9] Each of these has a traditional letter name.

Table 5.1

Name	Type	Model	Example
A	Universal – Affirmative	All S are P	All students are kind.
E	Universal – Negative	No S are P	No students are kind.
I	Particular – Affirmative	Some S are P	Some students are kind.
O	Particular – Negative	Some S are not P	Some students are not kind.

A categorical syllogism features three categorical propositions: a *major premise*, a *minor premise* and the *conclusion*. It also contains three terms and only three terms, each term being used twice.[10] Here is an example:

All M are P.   (major premise)
Some S are M.   (minor premise)
Some S are P.   (conclusion)

The term that appears in the predicate of the conclusion is the *major term* (P) and also appears in the major premise. The term that appears in the subject of the conclusion is the *minor term* (S) and also appears in the minor premise. The term that appears in both premises but does not appear in the conclusion is the *middle term* (M). In standard form the major premise is listed first.

Since each categorical syllogism has three categorical propositions and there are four possible types of propositions, that means there are 256 possible forms of categorical syllogisms. Yet amazingly only twenty-four of these are valid. That is because they must conform to the six rules of valid inference for categorical syllogisms:

---

[9] Each of these categorical propositions is in standard logical form, meaning they each contain a quantifier ("all," "no" or "some"), a subject term, a copula ("are" or "are not") and a predicate term. We commonly use categorical propositions, although we do not always state them in standard logical form. Singular propositions are not usually stated in standard logical form but are treated as universals. "Steve went to the store" is an **A**-type proposition (universal-affirmative), and "Steve did not go to the store" would be an **E**-type proposition (universal-negative).

[10] The term must be used in the same sense throughout the entire argument.

(1) The middle term must be distributed at least once in the premises.[11]

(2) If a term is distributed in the conclusion, it must be distributed in the premise.

(3) No conclusion can come from two negative premises.

(4) If one premise is negative, then the conclusion must be negative.

(5) If both premises are affirmative, the conclusion must be affirmative.

(6) If both premises are universal, the conclusion cannot be particular.[12]

Argument (d) is guilty of breaking the first rule. The term *male* is the middle term and is undistributed in both of the premises. Hence the argument is invalid. One evaluates a categorical syllogism by testing it by these five rules. If the syllogism breaks one or more of the rules, it is invalid. If it does not break any of the rules, then it is valid. Understanding the rules of the categorical syllogism and how they are employed takes a bit of practice and is beyond the scope of this chapter to cover in any detail.[13]

The second kind of syllogism is the *disjunctive syllogism*. A disjunctive syllogism makes use of the *disjunctive proposition*. A disjunctive proposition is an either/or statement that affirms or denies something in terms of two alternatives called *alternants*, as in the following example: "Either it rained last night or I left the sprinkler running." This proposition offers two alternative possibilities about what happened. In a valid disjunctive syllogism, one will deny one of these alternatives in the second premise and affirm the other alternant in the conclusion:

(k) Either it rained last night or I left the sprinkler running.
     I did not leave the sprinkler running.
     Therefore, it rained last night.

---

[11] A term is distributed if it refers to every member of a class. A term is undistributed if it refers to only some members of that class. In the proposition "All apples are fruit" the subject (apples) is distributed because we are referring to the entire class of apples. However, the predicate (fruit) is undistributed because we are not talking about the entire class of fruit, just those fruit that also happen to be apples.

[12] Different logicians list these rules differently, and so the numbers vary between five and six rules.

[13] Another way of checking categorical syllogisms involves the Venn diagram method, which uses three overlapping circles (corresponding to the three terms of the syllogism) to capture the logic of the premises visually. If inspection reveals that the information of the conclusion is then contained in the diagram, the syllogism can be said to be valid; otherwise it is invalid.

The logic of this kind of argument can be seen as a process of elimination. If I have only two possibilities and I take one away, then the other must be true. Assuming the first premise is true, only two possibilities obtain.[14] Assuming the second premise is true, I have removed one of the possibilities. Therefore, the conclusion is the only option left and must be true.

The disjunctive syllogism is less complicated than the categorical syllogism, as there is only one rule. The rule states: One must deny one of the alternatives in the second premise and affirm the other alternative in the conclusion. Argument (*k*) followed this rule and is valid. However, what if we were to do this:

(*k'*) Either it rained last night or I left the sprinkler running
      It rained last night.
      Therefore I did not leave the sprinkler running.

This syllogism is invalid. The reason is that my disjunctive proposition is inclusive, meaning it is possible that both alternatives could have happened: it could have rained *and* I could have left the sprinkler running. Therefore, affirming one of the alternatives in the second premise does not get me to any conclusion, because they can both be the case. (*k'*) is guilty of committing the *fallacy of affirming the alternant*.[15]

The third kind of deductive syllogism is the *hypothetical syllogism*, which employs the *hypothetical proposition*. A hypothetical proposition is a statement that affirms or denies something in terms of an *antecedent*, expressed as an "if," and a *consequent*, expressed as a "then."

Here is an example:

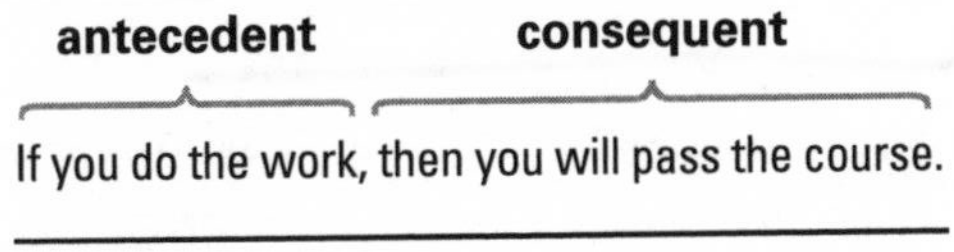

This proposition is making a promise or guarantee. If you do the work, whatever that in-

      antecedent   **consequent**

If you do the work, then you will pass the course.

Figure 5.1.

---

[14] If there were actually more than two alternatives then the proposition would be false.

[15] This rule is not to deny that there are exclusive disjunctive propositions, such as the law of excluded middle. Sometimes there are only two possibilities where the case must be one or the other and both cannot be true. For example, a person must be dead or alive. She cannot be both and must be one or the other. However, when used in a disjunctive syllogism the rule still holds that one denies one of the alternants in the second premise and affirms the other alternant in the conclusion.

volves, then you will definitely pass the course. If this proposition is true, then it is impossible to do the work and fail the course. What happens if you do not do the work? Many logic beginners assume that this proposition necessitates that if you do not do the work, then you will fail the course. "After all," they reason, "if you do not do the work, then you will fail the course." The above proposition tells us only what will happen if you do the work. It is not claiming anything about what will happen if you do not do the work. It states a *sufficient condition* for passing the course. It does not state a *necessary condition* for passing the course.[16] A sufficient condition states that this is one way of accomplishing the task. However, there may be other ways to pass the course (cheating, bribing the teacher), in which case doing the work would not be necessary.

Understanding how a hypothetical proposition works is key to understanding the hypothetical syllogism. There are two basic kinds of hypothetical syllogisms: the *pure* and the *mixed*. The pure hypothetical syllogism uses only hypothetical propositions for the two premises and the conclusion:

(1)   If you do the work, then you will pass the course.
      If you pass the course, then you will graduate.
      Therefore, if you do the work, then you will graduate.

The reasoning is pretty apparent in the pure hypothetical syllogism: If A, then B. If B, then C. Therefore, if A, then C.

A mixed hypothetical syllogism employs a hypothetical proposition for the first premise but then uses categorical propositions for the second premise and the conclusion. The key factor in determining validity in a mixed hypothetical syllogism is what is transpiring in the second premise. There are two forms of valid mixed hypothetical syllogism. The first form is called *modus ponens* ("the way of affirming"). In this form the second premise affirms that the antecedent of the hypothetical is true. Assuming the hypothetical is true, if the antecedent is affirmed, then the consequent must also be affirmed. Here is an example:

[16]A sufficient condition can be changed into a necessary condition by placing the word *only* before the "If," as in "*Only if* you do the work, you will pass the course."

(m) If you do the work, then you will pass the course.

    You did the work.

    You passed the course.

If it is true that "if you do the work, you will pass the course" and "you did the work," then it must be true that you passed the course. It is impossible for the conclusion to be false if the premises are true.

Another valid form of the mixed hypothetical syllogism is called *modus tollens* ("the way of denying"). In this form the second premise denies the consequent of the hypothetical proposition. Assuming the hypothetical is true, if the consequent is denied, then the antecedent must also be denied:

(m^1) If you do the work, then you will pass the course.

    You did not pass the course.

    Therefore, you did not do the work.

Again this conclusion must follow. How do we know you did not do the work? Because if you had, you would have passed. The first premise guarantees it.

The two rules for the mixed hypothetical syllogism are either to *affirm the antecedent* or to *deny the consequent* in the second premise. The fallacies would be to do the opposite. Here are two examples:

(m^2) If you do the work, then you will pass the course.

    You did not do the work.

    Therefore, you did not pass the course.

This syllogism commits the *fallacy of denying the antecedent*. Since doing the work is only a sufficient condition for passing the course, it is possible that there may be other ways of passing. Consequently, knowing you did not do the work does not warrant the inference that you did not pass. The argument is invalid.

(m^3) If you do the work, then you will pass the course.

    You passed the course.

    Therefore, you must have done the work.

This syllogism commits the *fallacy of affirming the consequent*. Again, the first premise allows for the possibility of other ways to pass the course. Therefore, the conclusion does not follow that you did the work, as you may have passed some other way.

INDUCTION

Perhaps the best way to understand inductive logic is to contrast it with deductive logic. As we noted above, in a valid deductive argument, the conclusion follows necessarily from the premises. So, if the premises are assumed to be true, the conclusion *necessarily* must be true. It is impossible for the conclusion to be false. This is never the case for an inductive argument. In a strong[17] inductive argument, the conclusion only *probably* follows from the premises. That is, assuming the premises are true, the conclusion is only probable. It never follows necessarily as in deduction. This is the key distinction between the two kinds of reasoning. No inductive argument reaches a conclusion that is logically certain in the same way as a deductive argument—even if the premises are true.

An example might help. Suppose I have a class of twenty students and, as they are coming into class, I observe each student individually, noticing that each is wearing a red T-shirt. Eighteen students have arrived, all with red T-shirts, and I draw the conclusion, "Since the vast majority of students in this class are wearing a red T-shirt, probably the last two will come in wearing one as well." Can I be logically certain of this conclusion? No. Why not? Because to be logically certain means that, if the premises are true, it is impossible that I could be wrong. But that is not the case here.

The reason that deduction reaches logically certain conclusions is that everything in the conclusion is already contained in the premises. A valid syllogism is thus based purely on the structural relationship between terms in the premises. We do not even need to use words to determine whether a deductive argument is valid or not:

(n) All Z are N.
     All N are H.
     All Z are H.

---

[17]In induction we use the terms "strong/weak" rather than "valid/invalid."

The above argument is valid even though we are not told what the letters stand for. However, inductive arguments reach conclusions that are intended to go beyond the information contained in the individual premises. In our above argument each premise was of an individual student wearing a red T-shirt. However, the conclusion contained more information than each premise individually; it attempted to reach a conclusion about the last two students. Thus, arriving at an inductive conclusion cannot be achieved with the same logical certainty as a deduction.[18]

Another distinction between deductive and inductive reasoning concerns how the two kinds of arguments are evaluated. Deductive reasoning has only two possible evaluations: the argument is either valid or invalid. However, in evaluating inductive arguments a number of options are possible. In general the two major alternatives are strong or weak. A strong inductive argument is one where, assuming the premises are true, the conclusion probably follows. A weak inductive argument is one where, assuming the premises are true, the conclusion probably does not follow. Unlike deduction, these two alternatives admit of degrees of probability. The conclusion for a strong argument could be extremely probable, very probable, somewhat probable or a little probable. The same degrees are possible of weak arguments.

What renders an argument more or less probable depends on the quantity or quality of the evidence supplied in the premises. Arguments that have either a great deal of evidence or evidence of a higher quality will be stronger than those that do not. Suppose I tell you that McDonald's is serving free cheeseburgers today. You are skeptical, and so you ask for evidence of my claim. I say, "Because they served free cheeseburgers on this day last year." Now, assuming this is true, is it more or less probable that they are doing so today? Most would admit that the probability is pretty low. Just because something happened a year ago on this day is not enough in itself to claim it will happen today. So you ask

---

[18]That does not mean that certainty cannot be obtained in a looser sense. We often speak of "practical certainty." By this we mean as certain as we can be under the circumstances. If I am careful in my observation of the students in the class, I can say that I am practically certain that they are all wearing red T-shirts.

me for more evidence, and I tell you that someone I trust told me that they were serving free cheeseburgers today. That is a little better, but most would still be skeptical on the basis of such little evidence. This third person could be wrong. Suppose I then tell you that along with these two facts, I also read in the paper that McDonald's is serving free cheeseburgers because they are celebrating the founding of the restaurant today. At this point you would begin to take the claim seriously. Finally I take you to a McDonald's, where we order cheeseburgers and they do not charge us. Here you would probably say that I have provided you with enough evidence to evaluate the claim that McDonald's is serving free cheeseburgers today as highly likely. Is it certain? No, but all the evidence points in that direction, and you can feel confident of the claim being true.[19]

Inductive arguments are often said to reason from the particular to the general. Although this is often true, it is not always the case. In the argument about red T-shirts, we did argue from observing individual instances to a general conclusion about the class as a whole. However, one can also argue from one particular to another particular inductively, as in an analogy (see below). So while it is often the case that induction goes from the particular to the general, it is not always the case.

Like deduction, inductive arguments come in a number of different forms. Let us look at six of them. *Generalization* is probably the most common form of inductive reasoning. In this form a number of particulars are gathered and a general conclusion attained. The example of the red T-shirts employed this method. Here is another example: A large number of college students are individually observed. A significant majority of them made better grades after taking a course in college studying strategies. Therefore, it is probable that taking this course results in better grades. Because there are a number of variables that need to be taken into account, we cannot be certain of our conclusion. But assuming that this is the one factor these cases have in common, our conclusion is justified with some degree of probability.

<hr>

[19]It is still possible that my original claim might be false. They could send you a bill, or maybe they were not serving real cheeseburgers, or I may have secretly paid the cashier in order to deceive you.

A second form of inductive reasoning is the *analogy*. An analogy is a one-to-one comparison between two or more things or states of affairs. The analogy is successful observing *relevantly* similar particulars and can arrive at a probable conclusion based on that similarity. Suppose Gary buys a new 2012 Porsche 911 from the local dealer. It has a manual transmission with a six-cylinder engine and gets 26 mpg on the highway. Sal also buys a new car and gets the same make with the same features from the dealer. By analogy we can say that if Gary's car gets 26 mpg, then Sal's will probably get about the same. We are analogizing from Gary's car to Sal's car, and we can reach this conclusion because of the similarities of the cars concerning the issue under consideration: gas mileage. Analogies are successful only as far as the discussion concerns areas relevantly similar to the issue under consideration.

A third form of inductive reasoning is *predictions based on the probability calculus*. This form of argument makes a prediction about a future event based on our past experiences in light of current conditions. Meteorologists often reason this way. They study current local and regional conditions such as temperature, barometric pressure, wind speed and direction and then, based on previous experiences with these conditions, predict the weather over a period of time. The meteorologist cannot be certain of her predictions (so do not blame her if she is off at times) because she may not know all the variables in play. She can predict only on the basis of what she does know. Hence she will usually express predictions in terms of percentage: "There is an 80% chance of rain on Tuesday." Predictions are often made in other areas as well, such as the stock market and the outcome of a football game. All these use inductive reasoning.

A fourth form of inductive reasoning is *statistical reasoning*. This occurs by gathering information from a sample population and attempting to extrapolate general trends, averages and percentages based on principles of statistics. Statistical reasoning plays a large part in scientific, psychological and academic studies, but most of us encounter it in the use of polls. A newscaster might say, "The president's approval rating rose by 8 percent last month according to a new *Wall Street Journal* poll." Some erroneously assume this means that 8 percent of all adult citizens think more highly of the president than in the previous months. However, the *Wall Street Journal* did not arrive at that number by polling the entire adult population of the United States.[20] A typical national poll usually considers eight hundred to one thousand people. The polling firm determines a sample population, asks their views about the president and then extrapolates from the sample what the whole country is thinking. The key to a successful extrapolation depends on a number of factors, including the size and representation of the sample, the phrasing of the questions and the manner in which the report is expressed. Statistical reasoning is a useful and effective way of arriving at an inductive conclusion, but one should cautiously examine the method and means of a particular poll or study, verifying that it was carefully done according to proper rules and guidelines. It is often said that numbers don't lie, but they can be misused and even distorted to mislead people into believing conclusions that are not necessarily true.

A fifth form of inductive reasoning is the *causal inference*. This is done by observing an effect and attempting to reason back to its cause. For example, if I attempt to start my car and nothing happens, I reasonably infer my battery is dead. The reason this is the first assumption is that in the experience of most people it is the most common reason the engine will not turn over. Other reasons are possible, such as the starter motor not functioning, but they are less common. I form a hypothesis as to what caused the effect, and then I test the hypothesis. Once I remove one possible alternative, I move on to the next. I remove the other possible alternatives and arrive at the cause. This is sometimes referred to as the scientific method or as hypothetical reasoning.

A final form of inductive reasoning is an *argument based on authority*.[21] The evidence cited to support a conclusion is some form of authority. It can be a person, an authoritative writing or an authoritative sign. For example, if you are driving down the road and you see a sign saying that there is a left curve ahead, it is reasonable to believe the sign because signs are generally reliable. It is always possible they can be wrong, but

---

[20] At the time of this writing, about 234 million adult citizens.
[21] However, there is no one kind of scientific method. Science broadly employs several methods to arrive at conclusions.

experience informs us that is the exception, not the rule. When it comes to persons and writings, more caution is advised. We recognize experts in some areas, such as science or history, but in other areas, such as politics, religion and ethics, we do not recognize definitive experts. For example, just because John Stuart Mill wrote a lot about ethics does not mean that he is an expert at what would be the right thing to do in a particular situation. It is recognized that there are many different views in these areas and therefore there is no one expert to appeal to for the definitive answer. Also, while an individual might be an expert in one area, such as science, that does not make him an expert in other areas, such as philosophy. Finally, even qualified experts can be wrong. Their testimony can add evidence for a conclusion, but caution is advised about arriving at a conclusion purely because someone says it is the case.

We looked at a number of fallacies under deduction. These are sometimes referred to as *formal fallacies*, for the error is usually structural. Fallacies also exist for inductive reasoning. They fall under the category of informal fallacies and will be covered in the next chapter.

Addendum

EXERCISES

Logic is a skill, and skills are learned by practice. Below are some exercises to help you better grasp the material covered in this chapter. Answers are at the end of the book. For each exercise, try to identify the following:

- What type of argument is it: deductive or inductive?

- What the form of the argument? If deductive, is it a categorical, disjunctive or hypothetical syllogism? If inductive, is it a generalization, analogy, prediction, statistical reasoning, causal inference or argument based on authority?

- If deductive, is it valid or invalid? If inductive, is it strong or weak?

1. Lisa is a student who understands logic.
   Some students who understand logic will get an A.

Therefore, Lisa will get an A.

2. The burglar must have been a tall, heavy man. His footprints sink an inch into the dry soil, and he wears a size fourteen shoe. Also, we found blood and hair on the rafter where he appears to have bumped his head.

3. If Chicago is a city in Illinois, then the Yankees will win the pennant. Chicago is a city in Illinois.
   Therefore the Yankees will win the pennant.

4. Either Dana went to the movies or he went to the library.
   Dana did not go to the movies.
   Therefore he went to the library.

5. This clay tile is the exact same brand, manufacturer and model of tile I laid on my patio last summer. Since the tile on my patio scratches very easily, it is likely that this tile will scratch easily. I wouldn't advise you to buy it.

6. The Green Bay Packers have won seven out of their last eight games, and the Detroit Lions have not won a single game all season. But the Lions can't keep losing forever. Therefore the Lions will probably beat the Packers in this Sunday's game.

7. If deism is true, then the Bible is false.
   But deism is false.
   Therefore, the Bible must be true.

8. I went out to my car this freezing cold morning and I could not get it to start. My neighbor's teenage kid probably poured sugar into my gas tank.

9. All animals who speak French have good artistic talent.
   My dog Toby speaks fluent French.
   Therefore, Toby has good artistic talent.

10. If objective morality exists, there must be a God.
    Objective morality exists.
    Therefore, there must be a God.

11. Dr. Jones, the eminent physicist, believes in psychic phenomena like ESP and ghosts. Given his expertise as a physicist, we should believe

in such phenomena as well.

12. In a recent poll of seven thousand college students on a variety of campuses across the country, it was discovered that a large majority of them began drinking alcohol while in high school. It appears that we may have a serious teenage drinking problem in this country.

13. Either Phyllis will go to the conference or Stuart will attend.
Phyllis is going to the conference.
So Stuart will not attend.

14. If this syllogism commits the fallacy of affirming the consequent, then it is invalid. This syllogism does not commit the fallacy of affirming the consequent. Therefore, this syllogism is valid.

15. Most of the students attending Liberty University are Christians. Kelly is a student at Liberty University. Therefore it is likely that Kelly is a Christian.

six

INFORMAL FALLACIES

A number of years ago I was walking along the streets of New York City when I came to a street magician performing card tricks before a small crowd. I stopped to watch and became fascinated with his sleight-of-hand abilities. At one point he turned to me and asked if I would like to play a game. The game was called three-card monte and was simple to play. He pulled out three cards; two were jokers, and the third was the ace of spades. He allowed me to examine the cards, and I noticed there was nothing special about them except for a slight bend lengthwise down each card that allowed one to easily pick up the cards when they were laid down on the table. He laid the cards face up in a row, with the ace in the middle.

"Now," he said, "this is an old con game where the innocent spectators often lost their money betting against the dealer. We are not going to do any betting, but I will show you how the game was played. I am going to turn the cards over and mix them up a bit. After I am done, all you have to do is tell me which one is the ace." I felt pretty good about my powers of observation and figured I could beat this guy, so I agreed. He flipped the cards over and began quickly shuffling them around on the table. I watched carefully, keeping my eye on the center card as it moved around the table. After a few seconds of shuffling he stopped, lined up the cards in a row and asked me to choose the ace. I felt confident that I had followed his movements and pointed to the card on the right. He asked me to turn it over. I was wrong—it was one of the jokers. The ace was on the left.

"The first time is always the hardest," he said. "Now that you have seen it, let me do it for you again." Again he turned the cards over, and again I watched carefully as he shuffled them around. When he stopped this time, I was sure I had the correct card. "It's in the middle," I proclaimed. When I turned it over, I was again disappointed to see a joker. The ace was on the right this time.

He then said, "I will do it one more time real slow. See if you can follow the ace." I was sure if he went just a little slower I could catch him. He flipped over the cards, but this time he shuffled them slowly around the table. I was amazed at how slowly and deliberately he moved the cards. I remember thinking, "Oh, this is just too easy." I effortlessly followed the ace, and when he stopped shuffling, I reached down triumphantly and turned over . . . a joker. I stood there staring at the card in my hand as the group of spectators laughed at my misfortune. I could not believe he had fooled me again. I knew he was doing some sort of sleight of hand, but for the life of me I could not discern what it was.

Informal fallacies are a little like that. We know something is wrong, but it is not always easy to discern where the error lies. In chapter five we examined some fallacies of deductive logic. Deductive fallacies occur when a specific rule of valid inference is broken. These are called formal fallacies because they break a formal rule. However, some fallacies do not break a formal rule, yet there is still something wrong with the reasoning. These are called *informal fallacies*. Whereas formal fallacies concern structural relationships, informal fallacies are often more concerned with the content of the argument. Observe the following argument:

(a) The Indian is a vanishing American.
That man over there is an Indian.
That man over there is vanishing.

If you were to apply the rules of valid inference to this categorical syllogism, it would seem to be valid, as it appears to keep all of the rules. We know, however, that this cannot be a valid syllogism because it does not make sense. The fallacy committed here is not a formal fallacy but an informal fallacy.

It is not easy to provide a precise definition of informal fallacies, but several standard ones have been identified. In general they fall into one of the following four categories: fallacies of weak induction, fallacies of presumption, fallacies of ambiguity and fallacies of relevance. Let us look at some classic examples of each of these.

Fallacies of Weak Induction

In this first group of fallacies, an error arises because the reasoning between the premises and the conclusion is inductively weak and leads us to a conclusion that may be presented as strong but does not follow.

Hasty generalization. As the name implies, this fallacy occurs by arriving at a conclusion on the basis of insufficient evidence. Hence our conclusion is arrived at hastily. In chapter five we discussed the inductive method of generalization, in which a number of particulars are gathered together and a general conclusion is obtained. The success of that method depends on gathering an adequate representative sample from which we can reach a conclusion. In hasty generalization, our representative sample is qualitatively or quantitatively inadequate to reach any conclusion. Here is an example:

Years ago I owned a Ford, and I always had problems with it. My dad also owned a Ford when he was younger, and he told me it was always in the shop getting fixed. The conclusion is obvious: Ford makes nothing but lemons.

Considering how many automobiles Ford sells a year—more than two million in 2011—and the lengthy time frame involved in this argument, it is highly unlikely that a conclusion can be reached on the overall quality of Ford automobiles on the basis of two cars, both of which were manufactured some years ago. This conclusion is too quick and based on insufficient evidence, so the argument is weak.

Accident or sweeping generalization. The fallacy occurs by applying a general principle to a specific case to which that principle does not apply. This fallacy often results from a tendency to confuse general principles with hard-and-fast absolutes and then apply these to each

---

[1]The Latin name for this fallacy is *dicto simpliciter.*

and every case without considering possible exceptions. This is not to deny the existence of absolutes, but it is to recognize that some principles were never meant to be taken as such. This fallacy sweeps everything together without taking into account relevant distinctions that make a difference. Note the following examples:

The Constitution guarantees freedom of religion. Therefore the Church of Divine Enlightenment, which practices child sacrifice, should have the freedom to continue with its unique form of worship.

Property should be returned to its rightful owner. Therefore you should give your drunken friend's car keys to him when he asks for them.

Running is good exercise. Therefore everyone should run several miles a day.

All of these contain good general principles, but they are not absolutes. Some forms of worship might be immoral or illegal, and our constitutional guarantee was not designed to support such activities. A right to private property is a good principle, but there are situations that justify overruling that right. And running is good exercise, but some people should not participate in so strenuous an activity.

Well-intentioned Christians can be notorious at committing this fallacy. Some will often take a scriptural principle and turn it in to an absolute promise. Parents claim the promise of Proverbs 22:6 (KJV), "Train up a child in the way he should go, and when he is old, he will not depart from it," only to be disappointed when their child becomes rebellious. Part of the problem is that they are treating a proverb as if it is a promise. Proverbs are bits of wisdom that, if followed, typically lead to good consequences, but they are no guarantee, and treating them so leads to the fallacy of sweeping generalization.

Weak analogy. As we noted in the previous chapter, an analogy is a comparison between two or more things or states of affairs. The success of an analogical argument depends on the *relevant* similarities between the items being compared. A weak analogy occurs when the items being compared are not relevantly similar concerning the issue under consideration. They might be similar in some respects, but they are not similar enough relevant to the issue. Look at this example:

Consumers, who pay for their purchases, get to select what they want when shopping based on their own personal preferences. Therefore college students, who pay for their education, should be allowed to pick which courses, assignments and tests they want to take based on their personal preferences.

While it is true that consumers and college students are similar in that they both are paying for what they are receiving, that is where the comparison ends. Shopping and getting an education are very different. In getting an education students are often unaware of the material they need to learn and what is involved in understanding it. So they need experts, like college professors, to guide them in selecting courses, fulfilling assignments and evaluating them on their progress. This is hardly the same as buying a pair of shoes. Should you encounter an argument based on analogy, ask yourself, "Is the comparison based on a *relevant* similarity?"

False cause. This fallacy is committed when we attempt to draw a causal inference between two events and there is little evidence that the two events are causally connected. One version of this is the well-known *post hoc*[2] fallacy. In this version of the fallacy, an individual mistakenly concludes that because one event occurred temporally after another event, the first event must have caused the second. Many of us have heard people say, "I knew it would rain. I just washed my car." Of course few of us take such claims seriously—washing cars has nothing to do with precipitation. However, it is not uncommon for a person to draw a causal inference between two events without providing evidence and therefore be guilty of the *post hoc*:

Studying philosophy will cause you to lose your faith. I know that because my brother Mike took a course in philosophy at college. Soon afterward he dropped out of school, stopped going to church and got heavily into drugs.

Asserting that philosophy was the cause of Mike's decline does not follow. There may be many reasons why he changed. To select philosophy as the sole reason he changed simply because he studied it before he adopted these behaviors provides no evidence that it was the cause of his change. Here is another example:

---

[2]Short for *post hoc ergo propter hoc* ("after this, therefore because of this").

Christianity is just a myth built on earlier pagan myths that also had some sort of savior-god who was "born from a virgin" and "rose from the dead."

There are a number of problems with this common criticism of Christianity, the main one for our purposes being this: because an earlier religion may have similar claims to Christianity does not by itself constitute evidence that the cause for Christian beliefs is that earlier source.[3]

A second type of false-cause argument is the *oversimplified cause.* Often there may be more than one cause for an event, or it may be the result of a causal series. Care needs to be taken that we do not reduce a complex problem to a simplistic cause. The argument about Mike above is a good example. The causes for a dramatic change in Mike's lifestyle are probably due to a number of social, psychological and moral concerns. It is naive at best to identify just one cause for such a complicated problem. The tendency to oversimplify, as lamentable as it is, is rampant in a culture that continually reduces complex ideas to thirty-second sound bites.

A third type of false-cause fallacy is the *non causa pro causa* ("not the cause, for the cause"). This fallacy occurs when something that is not the cause is inferred as being the cause for an event or effect with no evidence offered to support the inference. Unlike the *post hoc* fallacy, this version of the fallacy does not involve temporal succession. For example, oftentimes things are mistakenly causally related when there is little relation between them:

No wonder there are random acts of violence in our schools today. Just look at all the violent video games out there and the amount of violence on television and in the movies.

It may be the case that there is a causal connection between violence in the media and violence in our schools, but evidence and an argument are needed to establish a causal connection. Just because both involve violence is not enough in itself to support the inference that one caused

[3]See Mark W. Foreman, "Challenging the Zeitgeist Movie: Parallelomania on Steroids," in *Come Let Us Reason,* ed. Paul Copan and William Lane Craig (Nashville: B & H Publishing, 2012) for a refutation of this erroneous argument. The examples that are often cited of pagan religions having similar teachings and beliefs are spurious and grossly misunderstand what these pagan religions taught. At best the similarity is purely surface.

the other. Perhaps they are both caused by a third entity, such as an overall moral decline in modern society. Another type of the *non causa* fallacy is when cause and effect are interchanged:

The students who best understand the material will get the best grades. Therefore if we give Bill a high grade then he will understand the material.

The mistake in this case is confusing the cause with the effect. Being a good student causes one to get high grades, but getting high grades does not cause one to be a good student.

Slippery slope. The slippery-slope fallacy is usually considered a fallacy of its own, but it can be seen as a type of the false cause fallacy. It is a weak inductive argument that claims that given one event, an alleged chain of events will follow, but it offers little or no evidence to support such a claim. In most cases it is claimed that the chain will result in some disastrous consequence. This is an example of superlative arguing. The arguer attempts to make a case by arriving at an extreme conclusion that often overstates the actual situation. The key characteristic in the slippery-slope argument is its successive step-by-step development. Here is an example:

If a person gives up his belief in the inerrancy of the Bible, it won't be long before he stops believing in inspiration. If he stops believing in inspiration, he will begin to question all his religious beliefs. He will begin to doubt in God's existence. The end result will be that he will become an atheist and a moral reprobate.

Such an outcome *might* occur should a Christian deny inerrancy, but it is not inevitable. Many Christians have questioned inerrancy and arrived at a different outcome from the one suggested here. Slippery slopes are notorious for predicting unwarranted extreme outcomes.

Not all slippery-slope arguments are fallacious. If you can demonstrate a causal relationship that has strong evidence supporting a series of events leading to an outcome and you are careful not to overstate the case, then this would be a good argument. Scientists often predict the outcomes of a series of events this way, which is an acceptable form of arguing. It is a question of how much evidence you have and how precise and principled you are in employing it to reach a conclusion.

FALLACIES OF AMBIGUITY

Fallacies of ambiguity are a family of fallacies arising from language problems. The language employed might be unclear, vague, ambiguous or inappropriate in some other sense. Since philosophers seek clarity in presenting and evaluating arguments, they value language that is precise and accurate in expressing ideas. Here are some fallacies of ambiguity.

Equivocation. This fallacy occurs when the meaning of a significant term changes in the middle of an argument and thus distorts and usually invalidates the conclusion. In the English language we have a number of terms that can have more than one meaning. For example, think of the many meanings of the word *trunk*: the back of a car, the bottom of a tree, the snout of an elephant or a large crate in which one would pack clothing. Because of the flexibility of English, it is easy to begin an argument with a term having one meaning and to use the same term with a different meaning later in the argument. The fallacy about the Indian as a vanishing American at the beginning of this chapter is an example of this fallacy. There are two equivocations in that example. First, the term *vanishing* changes in meaning from a figurative to a literal use, and, second, the term *Indian* changes from a class distinction to a particular reference. Here are some other examples:

A woman has a legal right to an abortion. Therefore it is perfectly right for Susan to abort her unborn child.

Investigative Reporter: "People often accuse me of being sensationalistic. Well, I happen to think there are some stories that are pretty sensational."

Some argue that the publication of pornography is not in the public interest. However, I know many persons who are very interested in viewing pornography.

Probably fewer words are more often equivocated than the word *right.* In the example above, there is a significant difference between an action being the right thing to do (a moral concept) and one having a legal right to something (a legal concept). The two uses of "right" do not mean the same thing. In the second example, "sensational" means "highly unusual" while "sensationalistic" means treating something that is usual as if it is highly unusual. Finally, in the last example, the term "public interest" means what is best for the welfare of the public at large, but we all know that because of our weakness and fallen state, we are often interested in things that are not in our best interest.

Hypostatization. This fallacy occurs when one treats an abstract word as if it were a concrete word. Concrete words refer to particular objects such as the round *table*. Abstract terms refer to general qualities such as *roundness*. The most common form of this fallacy is through personification, or the attributing of personal characteristics to nonpersonal things. In hypostatization the nonpersonal things that are personified are abstract concepts. This may be an accepted practice in literature and poetry, but it is fallacious in argumentation because it introduces a certain amount of vagueness and distortion into the argument. Here is an example:

It is perfectly legitimate to eliminate the mentally feeble from society through eugenics. For just as nature in her mercy selects the fittest to survive and eliminates the lame, so we too are merciful helping nature in her process of keeping society fit.

"Nature" is a common theme employed in this fallacy. Nature does not have the ability to select or be merciful; only persons do. This might make for good poetry, but it distorts the argument to employ such language, and the result is a questionable conclusion. Another abstract term commonly personified is *culture*, as in "Morality is culturally determined." In truth culture cannot determine anything. *Culture* is an abstract term used to describe the general beliefs and practices of a community of persons. *Culture* may describe the way a community acts, but it does not prescribe how a community should act. Other abstract terms that are often employed in this fallacy are *science, society, government* and *truth.*

Amphiboly. An amphiboly is a well-known fallacy that is usually the result of ambiguous grammatical construction or poor sentence structure that introduces a lack of clarity in the sentence. One of the most common versions of this fallacy occurs when the referent of a pronoun is not clear: "Paul told David that he was mistaken about his solution to the problem." The difficulty here is that one is not sure to whom the pronoun "he" is referring. Was Paul telling David that Paul himself was mistaken, or was Paul telling David that David was mistaken? Here is another example: "If you don't go to other people's funerals, they won't go to yours." It is not clear precisely who "they" are referring to in this sentence.

Amphibolies are commonly found in writings where brevity is necessary, such as signs, newspaper headlines and advertisements. We get little context in helping us figure out the meaning. They also often produce humorous effects. Here are some examples:

Toilet Out of Order . . . Please Use Floor Below

We Exchange Anything—Bicycles, Machines, Etc. Why Not Bring Your Wife Along and Get a Wonderful Bargain

Panda Mating Fails; Veterinarian Takes Over

Enraged Cow Injures Farmer with Axe

Two Sisters Reunited After 18 Years at Checkout Counter

Composition and division. These are two separate fallacies, but because the reasoning is similar in both, I will discuss them together. Composition and division are known as part/whole fallacies because it is erroneously assumed that what is true of one must also be true of the other. In the fallacy of composition, it is erroneously thought that what is true of each part of something must necessarily be true of the whole. This sometimes is true, but it is not necessarily the case. One has to look at the context of the argument to see whether the fallacy applies or not. Here is a clear example of the fallacy:

Each member of Chicago Cubs is a great baseball player. Therefore the Cubs must be a great baseball team.

Even if it is true that each member of the Cubs is a great baseball player, it does not necessarily follow that they are a great team. There is more to being a great ball team besides having individually great players. They must play well together. There is a property that is present in the team that is not present in each individual player: synergy. Synergy is the interaction of elements that when combined produce a total effect that is greater than the sum of the individual elements by themselves.

Division is a fallacy that makes the same error in the opposite direction. It erroneously assumes that what is true of the whole must also be true of each individual part. We can use a similar example to demonstrate this fallacy:

The Los Angeles Dodgers are a great baseball team. Therefore each individual member must be a great baseball player.

Again the conclusion does not necessarily follow. Many of us have played on teams where the team has done very well despite some weak players. Sometimes a few great players are enough to carry the team to victory.

One needs to approach this fallacy with some caution. It is not always obvious when the fallacy is being committed and when the reasoning is legitimate. If each and every part of a fence is white, then one can nonfallaciously argue that the entire fence is white. One needs to look at the context to see whether the fallacy is present or not. Many theists have argued that every part of the universe is contingent, so the universe as a whole must be contingent. If every contingent thing needs a cause, then the universe needs a cause. Some atheists have argued that this argument is guilty of the fallacy of composition, but whether or not it is depends on whether the universe is equal to the sum of its parts or is greater than the sum of its parts.

There are other fallacies that fall under the category of language issues that do not have specific names. One is the use of emotionally loaded and cliché language. People are often passionate about the beliefs they hold. This may cause them to use language that packs an emotional wallop but may not be accurate and may even be misleading in arguing for a particular view. For example, in debates about abortion we often hear proponents argue that if we repeal *Roe v. Wade* we will return to the days of back-alley abortions. This phrase is used to elicit an emotional response by painting a horrible picture in the minds of the listeners. Such a picture aims to distract the listeners from the real issue of whether taking the life of the unborn is morally appropriate.[4] Caution is

---

[4]This is not to deny that such abortions took place before *Roe v. Wade* and still may occur today. However, many forget that before *Roe v. Wade*, abortion was legal in about a third of the states in this country and the vast majority of abortions were performed in sanitized clinical conditions by qualified medical professionals.

vital in a culture in which emotional appeals are a common form of persuasion. Oftentimes it is warranted to pause, reflect and ask how accurate are the portrayals of the issue at hand.

Sometimes arguers will appeal to clichés, epithets and pithy sayings to sway an opponent in a particular direction. For example, on the question of the morality of homosexuality one is likely to hear the term *homophobia* used against those who have moral problems with the acceptance of homosexuality as a legitimate alternative lifestyle. Is this the appropriate term? A phobia is a psychological aberration which results in an irrational fear of something. By this description, homophobia would be an irrational fear of homosexuality or homosexuals. It may be true that there are genuine cases of homophobia, but one needs to be careful in making such a diagnosis in the absence of a qualified psychological assessment. One cannot claim that individuals are homophobic simply because they have moral problems with homosexuality. Most of us have moral problems with murder, but I have never heard anyone claim that it is because we are "murderphobic." What has happened is that the term *homophobia* has become a cliché. It is a rhetorical device meant to persuade the listener without contributing anything to the discussion concerning the morality of homosexuality. Clichés cannot stand in for well-thought-out arguments.

FALLACIES OF PRESUMPTION

What is the difference between an *assumption* and a *presumption*? Although the terms are often used interchangeably, there is a subtle difference between them. To make an assumption is to take something for granted without investigating it. For example, when I sat down at my computer to type this chapter, I did not investigate the chair to see whether it would hold my weight. I assumed that it would. A presumption is like an assumption with a small twist. Again I am assuming without investigation, but in the case of presumption an epistemic obligation exists that usually is not present with a simple assumption. We recognize that many assumptions are reasonable and are not in need of investigation. Imagine what life would be like if every time we were to sit in a chair we had to take the time to see whether it was constructed well enough to hold us.

We have enough experience with chairs to feel confident that they will hold our weight and do not feel the need for constant investigation. Some claims, though, should be investigated before we believe them, and to ignore this obligation is to be presumptuous. The fallacies of presumption occur when one is not given the opportunity to investigate all of the options in an argument because the argument has been framed and presented in such a way as to ignore, distort or evade certain facts that may have significant bearing on the argument.

Begging the question.[5] This may be the most well-known fallacy of presumption. In this fallacy the main question or premise under debate is never addressed. Instead, the arguer presumes the issue is settled or does not need to be addressed and arrives at a conclusion without presenting the premise or allowing others to examine it. A common form of the fallacy leaves out the key premise in an argument. Note the following examples:

Killing an innocent human person without just cause is murder. Therefore abortion should be illegal.

Most paraplegics do not have the ability to take their own lives. Therefore physician-assisted suicide should be made available for them.

In both of these examples presumptions are made that are key premises to the argument and should be presented and discussed. However, the manner in which the argument is presented leaves these key premises out and presumes that everyone is settled on these issues. In the first example, the hidden premise "Fetuses are human persons" is highly debated and needs to be addressed and defended.[6] In the second example, the hidden premise is "Suicide is morally acceptable for paraplegics." Again, that is open to debate and should be presented for discussion and debate.

Sometimes begging the question occurs when the conclusion merely restates a premise. This is often done by using different language when moving from premise to conclusion, thereby concealing the fallacy. By

---

[5] Also known by its Latin name, *petitio principii*.
[6] I strongly hold the position that the unborn is a full human person from from the moment of conception. However, the claim needs to be addressed and discussed in arguments defending the right to life of the unborn.

placing the conclusion in the premises the arguer presumes that the conclusion is true in order to prove that it is true. Note this example:

Capital punishment is justified for the crimes of murder and kidnapping because it is quite legitimate that someone be put to death for having committed such hateful and inhumane acts.[7]

Notice how the conclusion says the same thing as the premise. You might not see it until you analyze the terms: "capital punishment" = "putting someone to death," "justified" = "it is quite legitimate" and "murder and kidnapping" = "such hateful and inhumane acts." All this argument is saying is "capital punishment is justified for murder and kidnapping because capital punishment is justified for murder and kidnapping." No reason is offered for the justification of capital punishment. The conclusion is presumed to be true.

A third type of begging the question is the circular argument. In this form the premise itself needs justification, and the arguer justifies it by appealing to the conclusion:

We know the Bible is the inerrant Word of God because it says in 2 Timothy 3:16 that "All Scripture is inspired by God," and God cannot lie.

In his opinion on *Roe v Wade*, Justice Blackmun of the Supreme Court claims that the state has an interest in protecting fetal life only when that life can live outside the womb. This is because, we are told by him, prior to being outside the womb the fetus has no interests or rights.

Aristotle taught that the "good" is whatever the good man approves of, and you can tell a good man because he always approves of the good.

The first example is circular, as it is using the Bible as the inerrant Word of God to prove that the Bible is the inerrant Word of God.[8] In the second argument Justice Blackmun is using the fact that the fetus has no interests or rights to prove that the fetus has no interests or rights. In the final example the argument is circular because in order to find a good man I have to know what the good is, and I can know that only by

---

[7]This example is from Patrick Hurley, *Logic: A Concise Introduction*, 9th ed. (Belmont, CA: Wadsworth/Thompson Learning), p. 146.

[8]I hope you realize that invalidating this argument is not to deny the Bible as the inerrant Word of God. I am saying only that this argument does not make that case.

knowing what a good man approves of, but I can know that only when I find a good man.

Bifurcation. This fallacy is sometimes referred to as the *false dilemma* or the fallacy of extremism. The fallacy occurs when we are presented only two possible options, usually extremes, when other options are possible. The fallacy presumes the two options are the only ones and does not allow us to consider other possibilities. It is common to see this fallacy employed by politicians, especially in the present climate of extreme partisanship:

Either you support the president's policies concerning health insurance or you are not a loyal American.

It seems to most people that a third alternative is possible wherein one can disagree with the president and yet remain a loyal American. Disagreement hardly makes one disloyal. I grew up during the late 1960s when the country was divided over the Vietnam war. Extreme positions were often taken on both sides of the debate. You were labeled as either a hawk or a dove. A famous bumper sticker of the time declared, "My Country: Love It or Leave It." The idea is that if you were not 100 percent in favor of the war, then you had only one option: leave. However, other options were possible. You might show love of country by raising your voice in protest when you believe the country is going in the wrong direction. We see much of the same problem in current times. Today you are labeled as a member of either the religious right or the liberal left. Little concern is given other options. The fallacy of bifurcation flourishes in such an environment.

Bifurcation occurs often with extreme terms like *never* and *always*. But rarely are these two options the case in reality. When a person claims, "You never do anything right," she is bifurcating the issue. It is difficult to believe that anyone "never" or "always" does everything right. None of this is to deny that sometimes there are only two options. When that is the case, one is not guilty of this fallacy. For example, the law of excluded middle tells us that something either exists or does not exist. There is no middle ground. Similarly, a person can be either dead/alive or male/female. In these cases there are only two options. One is only guilty of the fallacy of bifurcation when there are more than two options but only two are considered.

Special pleading. This fallacy occurs when one applies a double standard without warrant: one standard for us and another for them. It is important to note at the outset that not all double standards are illegitimate. For example, I had different standards for my children at different stages of their development. When my eldest was sixteen she was allowed certain privileges that her much younger sister did not have. Similarly, faculty are allowed certain perks that students are not. Such double standards are warranted. Unless there are justifiable reasons, however, many double standards are not legitimate. This is a fallacy of presumption because a double standard is erected without justification. Some years ago I heard a conservative radio commentator lambast the "liberal media" for treating their readers like they were idiots by commenting on a presidential debate. "They think you can't figure out for yourself what is going on and that you need them to explain it all to you." Immediately after concluding his tirade he said, "Now let me tell you what really happened in that debate." That is special pleading: *They are treating you like idiots, while I am helping you to understand.*

The above example demonstrates a common way this fallacy is committed: through the use of pejorative and euphemistic language. To speak euphemistically is to put something in its best light, making it sound better that it may be. To speak pejoratively is the opposite: to place something in a negative light, making it sound worse than it is. Notice this example from S. Morris Engel's classic work on informal fallacies, *With Good Reason:*

> The ruthless tactics of the enemy, his fanatical, suicidal attacks, have been foiled by the stern measures of our commanders and the devoted self-sacrifice of our troops.[9]

Note the language: when we speak of the enemy we refer to his "ruthless tactics" that are "fanatical" and "suicidal." When we speak of our troops we call our tactics "stern measures" and the actions of our

[9]S. Morris Engel, *With Good Reason*, 6th ed. (Boston: Bedford/St. Martin's, 2000), p. 172. This is one of the best books written on informal fallacies.

troops as "devoted" and "self-sacrificial." There may in fact be little difference between the two actions. Here are some other examples that use the same device:

I firmly believe that if you weren't so stubborn, you'd agree with me.

Our group of citizens is being disturbed by that gang over there.

Your party is noisy. We are just being active.

I am thrifty. You are stingy.

Complex question. Our last fallacy of presumption occurs when a question is asked that contains two questions but is phrased so that the responder can give only one answer and is not allowed to address both questions separately. The result is that the responder may end up affirming or denying something he does not intend to. Some examples will help:

How long have you been beating your wife?

How many cookies did you steal from the cookie jar?

Were you being dishonest or just stupid when you claimed you didn't know about the crime?

In all of these examples the same presumption occurs: we presume that one question is true and attempt to get the person to affirm it by answering a different question. The first example presumes that the person beats his wife in asking him how long he has been doing so. It does not give the individual the option of denying that he is beating his wife. The second example is similar—the child is never given the chance to deny that she stole any cookies. Any answer will be an admission of guilt. The third example is an interrogative form of bifurcation. The person is offered only two options, either of which makes him or her look bad.

As you can imagine, the complex question is a favorite of lawyers, who often try to trick witnesses on the stand into admitting something that they would not admit if asked directly:

Why did you wipe your fingerprints off the gun after using it?

The way of handling a complex question is to question the question. Stop and ask yourself if there is more than one question being presented.

Then take the time to separate and answer the questions individually. Do not get trapped.

FALLACIES OF RELEVANCE

Our last group of fallacies both is the largest group and contains some of the most common fallacies. What binds this group together is that all of the fallacies employ premises that are irrelevant to the conclusion being proposed. They might appear relevant and are presented that way, but on close analysis the conclusion does not follow from the premises. Like many of the fallacies we have already encountered, these can be intentional or unintentional. Many times arguers are unaware of the irrelevancy of the premises to the conclusion. Sometimes they are aware of it and hope no one notices. There are many fallacies of relevance, but we will look at only a few well-known examples.

Ad hominem. In this fallacy the arguer attacks the opponent instead of the issue. *Ad hominem* is Latin for "against the man." The erroneous principle behind the fallacy is that bad persons cannot produce good arguments. Therefore, if I can show that an individual is bad in some sense, then I have given you a reason not to consider his argument because automatically it is a bad argument. However, the quality of the person giving an argument has nothing to do with the merit of his argument; it is irrelevant. There are three common forms of the *ad hominem* argument. First is the abusive form. In this form the personal character of the opponent is attacked:

Senator Baker has argued that we should approve legislation in favor of protecting a woman's right to choose to terminate her pregnancy. However, Baker is a left-leaning atheist who was recently caught in a scandal with his secretary. How can we take the arguments of such a man seriously?

Dr. Wilson argues that there is strong evidence that Jesus rose from the dead and that the Gospel accounts of the resurrection are substantially reliable. However, isn't she a member of the Pinewood Country Club, an organization known for its racist membership policies? Is she really the best person to be arguing about Jesus?

The first argument directly attacks the character of Senator Baker by claiming that because of his beliefs and practices his argument is not worth listening to. Obviously, though, Baker may still offer a good argument regardless of his beliefs and lifestyle. They are irrelevant to the strength of his argument. The second example attacks Dr. Wilson indirectly by associating her with something distasteful and then uses that association to discredit her argument. But the fact that she belongs to a group that may have questionable practices is irrelevant to the argument she has produced.

A second form of the *ad hominem* is the circumstantial form. In this version, the person's motives rather than his character are attacked. If the position he is arguing for happens to benefit him personally, then, it is claimed, that should discredit his argument.

Bill's argument that Deuteronomy 14:26 should be interpreted as sanctioning drinking alcohol should be rejected. He just wants to justify his lifestyle of partying and drunkenness.

This may be the motive for why Bill has argued for this interpretation of the passage. But even if that is true, it does not entail that his argument has no merit. Just because the conclusion of an argument personally benefits a person is no reason to discount it as a bad argument. The motives behind an argument are irrelevant to whether it is a good argument or not. Most of us argue for things that we strongly believe in and therefore could be accused of bias in favor of the conclusion we are advocating. But that does not mean that our argument is without merit. We must judge the argument on its own merits regardless of who is making the argument or the reason they might be making it.

A final form of the *ad hominem* is the *tu quoque* ("you also"). The idea behind this fallacy is that the person making the argument is guilty of the practice she is arguing against, so her argument is invalid. When I was a young teenager I decided to try smoking cigarettes and was caught by my parents, who sat me down and lectured me about the dangers and detriments of smoking. It was hard to see them across the table, as I was blinded by all the smoke from the cigarettes they were puffing away on as they lectured me. Naturally my immediate response was, "Your arguments obviously fail—look at how much you smoke yourselves." However, the fact that they did not follow their own advice does not mean that they did not have good arguments. We can all agree that we should practice what we preach, but the fact that we do not practice it does not mean that what we preach is wrong or invalid. The weakness of our will to do what we know is right does not discount good arguments that it is the right thing to do. If I were to argue for the sanctity of marriage and you were to discover that I had been involved in an affair, it does not discount my argument even though you could question whether I am the one who should be making it. It might make me inconsistent, but not my argument.

Ad populum. This fallacy appeals to the idea that if a position is popular, then that constitutes positive evidence that it must be right. *Ad populum* is Latin for "appeal to the people." The most common way this is done is by showing that a large number of people agree with a position and therefore you should also. This is a favorite with advertisers:[10]

Four out of five Americans choose Zest soda pop over its leading competitor. Eighty percent of Americans can't be wrong. Buy Zest today.

The number of people who favor a product has nothing to do with whether you should buy it or not. This fallacy is also a favorite in political campaigns:

Polls show that most Americans are overwhelmingly in favor of the president's performance over the last four years. Reelect the president and keep America strong.

Oftentimes a subtler version of this fallacy inverts the logic. Rather than appeal to the majority, it appeals to a select few. The idea is to appeal to our desire to be special and unique. Many of us are familiar with the advertisement "The few, the proud, the Marines." This form of the fallacy appeals to our vanity and tries to convince us to agree with the conclusion because doing so will include us as members of an elite class of individuals.

---

[10] Always remember that advertising is arguing. Companies are arguing that you should buy their product. Many of the commercials on television are based on fallacious reasoning. In fact, the most common place to find informal fallacies is in advertising. Advertisers are often completely aware of what they are doing. They just hope you are not.

Not everyone can understand these complex arguments for my position. However, a few of you are bright enough to get this and will see the force of my conclusion.

Mercedes-Benz. It's not for everyone.

A different type of the *ad populum* is the mob appeal. In this form of the fallacy, the crowd is whipped up into an emotional frenzy based on some noble ideal. The heightened emotions, along with group dynamics, carry the audience along. In all the turmoil they often stop listening and evaluating what is being said. This often occurs in large group meetings, such as political conventions or religious revivals, where a single individual is speaking. If the person speaking is on "our side," we will tend to go along with the crowd and unreflectively agree with almost everything the speaker says. I have observed speakers in front of large crowds of college students presenting terrible arguments and advocating highly questionable notions and have watched as these crowds rise to their feet, cheering and applauding. Yet I know that if they were to calm down and reflect about what was being said, most would be very hesitant to agree with the speaker. There is some truth to Ibsen's warning: the greatest enemy to the truth can be the majority.[11]

Red herring. In the days when fox hunting was common, one technique employed in training the hounds was to drag a red herring across a trail and attempt to throw them off the scent. That is what happens with this fallacy. The idea is to divert the attention of the listener by subtly changing the subject. As you can imagine, this is a favorite among politicians, many of whom exploit the approach, "Don't answer the question that was asked; answer the question they should have asked." Note how the technique might be used in a presidential debate:

Moderator: Senator, you have been accused of waffling on the issue of illegal immigration. At one point you seemed to be in favor of tighter restrictions but recently seem to be open to an amnesty program for illegal aliens already present in this country. Can you clarify your position for us?

---

[11]Henrik Ibsen, *An Enemy of the People* (1882).

Senator: Thank you for giving me the opportunity to do that. Let me just say that our country is the great melting pot of different cultures and nationalities. We have greatly benefited from the skills and talents of the many foreigners who have come to our shores, and we should welcome their innovation. If I am elected president I plan to establish educational programs for those who come to our great country seeking a new life in a land of great opportunity.

This example shows how this fallacy often works. Notice how the subject is subtly changed from illegal immigration to the subject of the values and opportunities for any immigrants coming to the United States. The effective red herring will select a subject that is subtly related to the original, thereby avoiding detection. This is a fallacy of relevance because the new subject is irrelevant to the original topic under discussion.

Straw man. The straw man fallacy is similar to the slippery slope and bifurcation in that it usually appeals to an extreme as part of its tactic, but it operates differently from those two fallacies. The fallacy occurs when one takes another's argument, distorts it to an extreme and then proceeds to tear down the distortion in the belief that the arguer has torn down the original argument. The distortion is called a straw man because it is a false imitation of the original argument. Note the following examples:

My opponent has argued for an increase of subsidies in the Medicare program. What he is really arguing for is socialized medicine and the nationalization of medical care. However, this would destroy any incentive in the private sector to provide quality care. We would go from having the best medical care in the world to having the worst. Clearly my opponent's arguments must be rejected.

Christians teach that all people are sinners and are in need of God's grace to get to heaven. However, the vast majority of people aren't murderers, thieves or rapists. Therefore, Christians are wrong to condemn most people to hell.

Both of these examples have distorted the original argument. In the first example, what was being proposed was an increase in Medicare. This was distorted into a more extreme position that the original arguer never intended. The distortion was then discredited. The original argument was neither addressed nor discredited. In the second example, the original argument is saying that sin keeps us from God. The arguer comments only about extreme sins and never addresses the issue of sin itself. In doing so he thinks he has defeated the original argument.

It is easy to confuse the straw man with the red herring, as they both deal with replies to original arguments. To avoid such confusion, keep this distinction in mind: The red herring avoids the original argument by changing the subject. The straw man distorts the original argument to an extreme and then destroys the distortion.

Appeal to pity. Our final fallacy is one that I encounter often. In fact, I have nicknamed it "the student's fallacy" because I observe students committing this fallacy so frequently. It is called appeal to pity because, rather than argue on the merits of the issue itself, a person makes an irrelevant emotional appeal meant to rouse sympathy for the person involved, diverting attention away from the real issue. Here are some examples:

I think you should pass this student on the final. I know she failed it badly and she really doesn't have a good understanding of the material. But she studied so long last night. If she fails it will be impossible for her to pass the course and graduate next week. Her parents have already paid for plane tickets to come to the commencement, and they can't get a refund. She is so ashamed and sorry she didn't do better. She's been in tears all day. Can't you just give her the points?

Your honor, I know my client is guilty of tax evasion. But he has been going through an extremely difficult time lately. He lost his job due to an injury, and his wife took the kids and left him. We need to find him not guilty and give him an opportunity to get back on his feet.

How can you say assisted suicide is wrong? I have watched three loved ones slowly die of cancer. They suffered through excruciating pain as they slowly deteriorated over time. Jesus said, "Blessed are the merciful." I think we need to heed his teaching.

One can sympathize in all three of these situations, for they are all emotionally difficult. However, the argument being made in each is irrelevant to the issue at hand. In the first example (which is more common than you can even imagine), while we can feel sorry for the student, the fact is that grades are supposed to reflect the student's understanding of the material in the course. Assuming the test is fair and well written, failing it informs us that the student does not have an adequate understanding of the material. The situation of failing the class, not graduating and the parents not being able to obtain a refund is irrelevant to the issue at hand, which is an adequate understanding of the material. In the second example, none of the aspects of the defendant's life has anything to do with whether he is guilty of tax evasion. The purpose of the court is not to help him get his life together; it is to render a verdict concerning tax evasion. Finally, the question of the morality of assisted suicide is not settled by being merciful. It involves questions of justifiably intending to end a person's life and the important question of a doctor's role in helping someone do that. While not denying the emotionally gut-wrenching experience of watching a loved one suffer, we cannot allow emotions to take control in such situations. Such complex issues need rational, reflective consideration.

Conclusion

I stood there looking at the card in my hand. I laid it on the table, stepped back and continued to watch the magician perform sleight of hand. His performance was mesmerizing. After he finished and the crowd was dispersing, I asked him to tell me how he fooled me. He told me that a magician never reveals his tricks. However, he could see how earnest I had become, and so he offered to teach me a simple vanishing coin trick. He told me never to perform the trick until I had practiced it enough to perform it flawlessly. He said that if I could master that trick, he would tell me where I could learn more. Many years later I learned how to do the three-card monte and have performed it over the years for friends. Sleight of hand taught me that, through practice, you can learn to master great abilities, including learning how to spot informal fallacies. I challenge you to read, listen and practice honing your ability not to be fooled. You will have no trouble finding examples, for, unlike street magicians, informal fallacies are all around us.

Addendum

Here is a list of the fallacies we covered in this chapter grouped together by type, followed by several exercises for each group. See whether you can identify any of the fallacies below.

Fallacies of Weak Induction

- Hasty generalization
- Sweeping generalization
- Weak analogy
- False cause
- Slippery slope

1. Third baseman Wade Boggs was so superstitious that he would eat chicken before each game and take batting practice at exactly 5:17 each evening before a night game. He ended up with a .328 career batting average, won five batting titles, collected more than 3,000 hits, played in twelve All-Star games, won a World Series and was inducted into the Baseball Hall of Fame on his first ballot. Following those superstitions really pays off.

2. Human beings have the ability to calculate numerical equations and process information, and they have basic rights. Computers can also calculate numerical equations and process information. Computers must have basic rights as well.

3. Our students are requesting that we reexamine our assessment policies. But if we begin down that road, where will it lead? Next they will insist we eliminate exams altogether. This will lead to the abolishment of our courses and programs. Soon the entire university process will be abolished. We must resist this movement by the students to destroy higher education.

4. She is the third student I have caught cheating this term. The obvious conclusion is that you just can't trust any of these students anymore.

5. The Constitution guarantees freedom of speech. Therefore, there is nothing wrong with someone crying "Fire!" in a crowded movie theater.

Fallacies of Ambiguity

- Equivocation
- Hypostatization
- Amphiboly
- Composition
- Division

6. Every word in Lincoln's "Gettysburg Address" is ordinary. Therefore his speech is ordinary.

7. It is greed that builds and improves the country's economy. If greed is left alone to do his job, wealth accumulates and the whole country is better off. If greed is impaired, then thrift takes over, and she will stifle growth. Leave greed alone. He will be kind to you in the end.

8. The verdict rendered by the jury was reasonable and just. Therefore Erin, who was a member of the jury, is a reasonable and just human being.

9. Did you hear that Paul has a picture of Jeannette hidden in his locker? I wonder how he was able to get her to fit in such a small space.

10. How can you doubt the miracles of the Bible? Every day we witness the miracle of a new birth.

Fallacies of Presumption

- Begging the question
- Bifurcation
- Special pleading
- Complex question

11. My sister really bugs me. She keeps going through my things and borrowing them without asking. The other day I found one of my sweaters in her drawer.

12. Philosophy instructors must be intelligent people because they wouldn't be philosophy instructors if they weren't intelligent.

13. How long have you been cheating in this class?

14. Either she knew everything that was going on, in which case she is a liar, or she was completely oblivious to what was going on around her, which makes her an idiot.

15. We better stock up with as much as we can, because the others will get here soon and you know how they hoard everything.

Fallacies of Relevance

- Ad hominem
- Ad populum
- Red herring
- Straw man
- Appeal to pity

16. Michael J. Fox has argued for an increase in funding for stem cell research. But Fox has Parkinson's Disease and is only arguing for stem cell research so they will find a cure for him. Therefore, we should reject his arguments.

17. My opponent argues that teachers are doing a poor job educating our children on the basics these days. However, the real problem in our schools is student attitudes and behaviors. Students are late to classes, show up in tattered jeans and T-shirts, and spend all their free time on Facebook and Twitter. They have no sense of self-respect and no discipline.

18. I think we should give the award for the best essay to Steve. He has had a rough time this year. He lost his mom to cancer, and his dad had to take on another job just to make ends meet. Steve tried out for the baseball team and didn't make the cut. I know his essay may not be the best, but I think winning this award is just the boost he needs.

19. The workers have argued that we need to improve the ventilation system in the factory. However, there is no way we can afford a

whole new air-conditioning system. It would mean all new duct work throughout the entire factory and three large new air conditioning units on the roof. The expense would be enormous. We will just have to reject the workers' arguments.

20. Anyone with half a brain believes in evolution today. Therefore, you'd be wise to go along.

seven

ANALYZING ARGUMENTS

I was a big fan of the television series *House*. For those unfamiliar with this series, it centered on one of the most iconic fictional characters ever created, Dr. Gregory House. House was an extremely intelligent medical doctor who headed the department of diagnostics at the fictional Princeton-Plainsboro Hospital. Every week he and his team would work on a particularly complex case to diagnose some rare disease exhibited by that week's patient. House would use his superior analytic abilities to arrive at a conclusion and treatment just in time for the end credits. I often use House as an illustration in my bioethics class because he was not only extremely intelligent but also notoriously unethical. As a matter of fact, he was one of the most immoral reprobates ever to don a lab coat. He regularly lied to his patients and colleagues, bragging that he was justified because "everybody lies." He constantly violated the rights of his patients with no regard for their beliefs or values, hurling insults at them as he treated them. His actions were often illegal and out of control. I describe him thus to my students and ask, "He's a fascinating fictional character, but how many of you would want House as your doctor?" Amazingly, a significant number of them raise their hands. Why? It is because of those incredible analytic abilities. The students affirm the message of the show week after week: we will tolerate incredibly childish and decadent behavior to have someone who can analyze and solve problems in the way that House can.

I was not surprised to learn that Gregory House was based in part on another fictional character known for his analytical abilities: Sherlock Holmes.[1] Holmes too had an uncanny ability to observe and analyze a situation and arrive at a conclusion. When queried by Watson as to how he arrived at his conclusions, he would famously say, "Elementary, my dear Watson, I deduced it." He would then explain step by step how he arrived at some remarkable conclusion. Watson would often respond that, as Holmes explained his steps, the reasoning was obvious. But before the explanation he was baffled by Holmes's abilities. In *A Study in Scarlet* Holmes explains, "In solving a problem of this sort, the grand thing is to be able to reason backward. That is a very useful accomplishment, and a very easy one, but people do not practice it much. . . . There are fifty who can reason synthetically for one who can reason analytically."[2] Practice was the secret in becoming a good analyst.

This last chapter is about analyzing arguments. I will approach our discussion from two perspectives. First I want to approach it from the perspective of constructing an argument, and then I want to offer a tactical approach to examining the arguments of others. With some practice, you can become as proficient as Holmes or maybe even House—sans the decadence. Let's begin . . . the game is afoot.

ELEMENTS OF A GOOD ARGUMENT

At some time or another all of us present arguments for ideas or beliefs that we hold. It may be in the formal setting of a paper or presentation for a class. You have been assigned a controversial topic and need to defend a particular position on it. It may or may not be your own position. Or the situation might be more casual, as in a conversation with some friends. You are talking over dinner and an issue comes up. Perhaps it is an ethical, political, theological or other social issue. There is some disagreement and debate over the topic. Perhaps you have some

[1]Minus the character flaws. It is no coincidence that House's confidant, Wilson, was designed to resemble Watson. One can even see the similarity in their names.

[2]Sir Arthur Conan Doyle, "A Study in Scarlet" (1887), in *The Complete Sherlock Holmes*, ed. George Stade (New York: Barnes & Noble Books, 2003), p. 93. For an excellent essay on Holmes and philosophy see David Baggett, "Sherlock Holmes as Epistemologist," in *The Philosophy of Sherlock Holmes*, ed. Phillip Tallon and David Baggett (Louisville: University of Kentucky Press, 2012).

strong beliefs, and those beliefs are being questioned by some person or persons. You attempt to defend your belief and recognize how inadequately prepared you are. So you later decide to do some research and prepare a better defense for the belief you hold. In either of these situations, you need to construct an argument. I would like to suggest nine elements that you should think through as you put your argument together. Although this is not meant to be a comprehensive list of the elements of a good argument, I believe it is a good start.

Good reasoning. Not surprisingly, the first element of a good argument is that it has good reasoning in it. Good arguments conform to the laws of logic. This means they will not contain contradictions. They will also maintain the rules of valid inference, the rules that govern deductive syllogisms, such as "affirming the antecedent in *modus ponens*." Good arguments avoid the informal fallacies we discussed in chapter six. This first element implies that you need to have an adequate understanding of these rules and fallacies. I encourage those of you who are planning careers in which arguing is a regular activity to consider taking a course or two in logic and critical thinking to sharpen your reasoning skills.

Clarity. This second element cannot be stressed enough. Good arguments are clear, accurate and precise. You need first to be clear in your own mind of what exactly it is you are defending. You need to be clear about the structure of your reasoning and how the premises lead to the conclusion. Second, you need to clearly communicate your thoughts and ideas to others. This involves using appropriate language that accurately expresses your ideas. It might mean taking the time to define significant terms so that everyone understands exactly what you are saying. If you watch good debates, the participants will often start by defining terms. This avoids potential problems when the argument becomes complex and one participant might equivocate on the terms in use. Striving toward clarity also means avoiding using emotionally loaded language and clichés. Such language introduces obfuscation into the argument. Above all you want to avoid the two great enemies of good arguments: vagueness and ambiguity.

Consistency and coherence. Consistency means that within a set of beliefs none of them contradicts the others. Within your arguments you may introduce a number of beliefs to support the premises employed in the argument. It is important that these beliefs are consistent with one another. Inconsistency is a sign of falsehood and introduces problems into the argument. Sometimes our beliefs are not really inconsistent, but they might appear so because they have been inadequately expressed. Not only do they need to be consistent, but also they need to be expressed in such a way that the consistency is apparent. However, consistency by itself is not enough. A good argument is more than a bunch of consistent beliefs. In good arguments, beliefs need to be related together, and that is the task of coherence. Coherence means that the beliefs relate together in a way that is mutually supportive. I believe that my life has meaning and purpose because Jesus loves me and he would not love a meaningless life. This is supported by my belief in God as an infinitely good and loving being, by my belief that Jesus is divine and by my belief that the Scriptures are substantially reliable in what they tell me about Jesus. Each of these beliefs is consistent *and* coherent with one another.

Comprehensive. Good arguments take all of the relevant facts into account and attempt to address all the known problems. This element recognizes an epistemic limitation: we rarely, if ever, have complete knowledge about an issue. In fact, one of the reasons many issues are open to discussion and debate is due to the lack of data at our fingertips. In an ideal world we might have all knowledge and then there would be no disagreement. Needless to say, this is not an ideal world. That being said, we want to be as comprehensive as we can. Good arguments consider all known reasonable alternatives and arguments for a view and can account for them as part of the overall argument. This does not necessarily mean that every alternative needs to be presented and addressed in your argument. The context will often determine how much needs to be brought up. In formal settings, such as presenting a paper among your peers, you will probably address more alternatives than in an informal conversation over coffee. However, a good argument should at least have an answer prepared for challenges and alternatives if raised.

Orderly structure. Good arguments are structured well; they are mapped out and presented in a form where the reasoning is apparent. As of this writing I have been teaching for about thirty years. I have read and graded thousands of student papers, many of which have been very good, but many of which have had serious difficulties. The most common problems I encounter are structural issues. Some papers have been such a mess that it is almost impossible to find any coherence in the paper. Premises, supporting issues and conclusions are all jumbled and confused. Part of the problem is that many people write like they converse. Conversation tends to be serendipitous. It will often jump from topic to topic with little structure. Many student papers do the same. Good arguments have an apparent structure to them that makes them fairly easy to follow.

There are a number of means to accomplishing good structure. Most arguments will take one of two basic approaches. They will either state the conclusion first followed by the premises, or they will state the premises and then follow with a "therefore" type of conclusion. Either of these is effective, though the first is more common in formal settings and the latter in casual settings. If the reasoning is complex, you might consider setting your premises apart by numbering them or employing some other designation. If the premises themselves need further support, offer it along with the premise as a subpoint. Make sure it is clear which subpoint goes with which premise, and avoid raising support for a premise much later on in the argument. In extremely complex arguments you may need to summarize your main premises at the end and relate them together in a formal arrangement like a syllogism.

Fair use of evidence. Good arguments use evidence fairly and avoid suppressing evidence in favor of a particular position. We all want to present the case for our view in its best possible light. In the process of researching and developing our argument we may run into problems and evidence counter to the view we support. We might be tempted to ignore or suppress that evidence. Perhaps we even hope our opponent will be ignorant of this evidence and it will not come up in the process of presenting our argument. However, if our goal is to arrive at the truth, then it is our obligation to examine all the evidence and account for it from our perspective. Good arguments do not have the option of being selective toward the evidence they consider. It all needs to be laid out in the open and considered. If there is a serious problem for the view you are supporting, then you need to seek for a way to account for that evidence if you are going to continue to maintain that view. It may be serious enough that you will have to amend or even abandon your position. Perhaps you cannot find a way to resolve the problem, but the evidence for your position is strong enough that you can still maintain the view you have and will leave this problem unresolved for now with the hope of resolving it in the future. The one thing philosophy does not allow you to do is to ignore it or suppress it in hope that it will disappear. It will not, and it is likely to rear its ugly head when you least expect it. It is always better to acknowledge honestly evidence contrary to your own view and deal with it up front. An additional advantage is tactical: it will usually take the wind out of your opponent's sail.

Positive/negative approach. Tactically, this is the strongest approach to take in presenting an argument. Good arguments not only present positive evidence in favor of the view they are supporting. They also provide negative evidence toward the view they are opposing. This can be direct evidence against that view or in the form of problems with the evidence that view employs. I recently viewed a debate between Sam Harris and William Lane Craig on the question, Is the foundation for morality natural or supernatural? In Craig's presentation of his case for the supernatural foundation for morality, he began by arguing in favor of his position and provided a number of reasons why he thought the existence of God accounts for objective moral obligations. However, he did not stop there. He then examined the case for naturalism and explained why the reasons Harris offered do not adequately support his conclusion that naturalism can account for objective moral obligations. Tactically Craig's argument was very strong. He was not just offering another view. He offered a superior one. If you offer an adequate defense for your own view without critiquing the other view, then the best you may be able to arrive at is a draw—both views may be equally plausible. However, if you can show that not only does your view have good evidence but also the opposing view is weak, then your argument is much stronger.

Best explanation. Rarely does any one argument answer every problem. It is important to remember that few controversial issues have perfect solutions with no problems. Almost every solution has some problems. The goal is not to find the perfect solution but to arrive at one you can live with, to discover which view offers the best explanation with the least number of problems. For example, I believe Christian theism explains certain facts in the world better than naturalism, such as the existence and design in the universe as well as consciousness and the presence of absolute moral obligations. However, I also recognize that there are aspects of Christian theism that are problematic and difficult to explain, such as why God allows specific evils to occur in the world or why he often appears as silent.[3] Despite these problems, I believe that naturalism is much more problematic than theism. Theism offers a better overall explanation than naturalism in explaining a number of aspects of the world we live in.

What does it mean to offer a best explanation? First, the best explanation will have the largest *explanatory scope*. Explanatory scope considers the quantity of facts accounted for by an explanation. The more facts accounted for, the more likely an explanation is correct. Second, the best explanation will have superior *explanatory power*. The explanation that can be understood with the least amount of effort, vagueness and ambiguity has the best explanatory power. You should not have to force facts to make them fit with the explanation. A third aspect of a best explanation is *plausibility*. This has to do with the explanation fitting with our background knowledge. The explanation that is more plausible given the background knowledge we already have is better than the one that seems implausible in accordance with background knowledge. A fourth condition is that the best explanation is *minimally ad hoc. Ad hoc* means an explanation that is created for the situation at hand. It is usually an explanation that would not generally apply but is necessary for this particular situation. It often employs the use of creativity and imagination to arrive at an explanation beyond what the evidence tells us. Generally *ad hoc* evidence is not looked on favorably and is viewed as an act of desperation. Therefore the explanation that is less *ad hoc* is considered the better one. Finally, the best explanation will have the property of *illumination*. By illumination we mean the ability of an explanation to provide light on related areas besides the question at hand.

---

[3] I believe there are plausible explanations for evil and silence, but I also recognize why many are perplexed by these problems.

Sometimes a best explanation not only will explain the particular question under consideration but also will address a host of related questions and issues. For example, the resurrection of Jesus does not just best explain the facts of reports of his appearances and the empty tomb, but also it supports his claims to deity and the other claims of the miraculous in his life. It is important to note that the best explanation or theory may not be perfect in these five elements. Sometimes we must settle for the best we have.

Principle of simplicity. Good arguments are those that do not contain unnecessary assumptions and reasoning. This element of a good argument, also referred to as *parsimony*, is usually traced back to the late medieval philosopher William of Occam. Occam developed a principle that states: Entities should not multiplied without necessity. He believed that many medieval philosophers had speculated about the existence of entities and principles that were bloated and unnecessary in explaining the world. For Occam, an explanation was usually the best when it did not contain unnecessary assumptions and baggage. He used this principle to cut away all of those ideas that he believed were not necessary and muddied the waters. It came to be known as Occam's razor. Although it is not exactly the same thing, today we often refer to the principle of simplicity by another term, the "kiss" principle: keep it simple, stupid.

There is much to be said for keeping ideas simple. In general a simpler explanation will often be the best one. However, you need to be careful in how you wield Occam's razor. The fact is, many issues are often more complex than we initially give them credit for. Care must be taken that in our striving for the simplest explanation we do not become simplistic. We already live in a culture that continually attempts to boil down complex issues into thirty-second sound bites. Many issues are enormously complex and need serious thought and reflection. I often cannot answer many of the multifaceted and intricate problems of philosophy with a naive, one-dimensional, quick response. Some simpler explanations may end up subtracting entities that are, in fact, necessitated. So this principle needs to be balanced: Keep your explanation as simple as is necessary while realizing that even the simplest explanation may need to be quite extensive and difficult.

ANALYZING ARGUMENTS: TACTICAL APPROACH

Along with producing arguments we also frequently encounter arguments from others. In fact, by sheer number, we encounter many more arguments than we create. Although we may not recognize them as such, arguments are thrust at us daily. We encounter them in the media through advertisements. Many of the movie and television programs we watch and the books we read are not just entertaining us but are also arguing for a particular point of view. Stories are the most subtle form of argumentation, as we are often not aware of the subliminal argument being made. If we are not careful, we might find ourselves affirming ideas that, if they were presented directly to us, we would never agree to.

In this second part of the chapter I want to present a strategy for analyzing the arguments we encounter. Naturally this strategy is somewhat general, as there are many different kinds of arguments out there. I believe that if you follow the steps I offer here, you will be on your way to understanding and evaluating many of the arguments you will come across as you continue to develop the philosophical mindset. In order to accomplish our goal, we need a sample argument to analyze. I will use a fairly simple one to start with and then will suggest some others as we go through our steps. Here is our argument:

Westminster College is the best small liberal arts college in the state. Their faculty is well prepared and professionally active. Also, the students come in with high scores on college aptitude tests, and most of them are successful in their professions after they graduate.

Step 1: Distinguish the premises from the conclusion. As we have discussed, the conclusion is the point the argument is trying to prove, and the premises are the reasons being offered to support why we should believe the conclusion is true. In order to analyze and evaluate the argument, we need to know which of these is which. So the first task in analyzing any argument is to find the conclusion. Sometimes the conclusion is obvious, and sometimes it is not. Here are three tactics to help you find the less-than-obvious conclusion. First, look for indicator terms. These are words that appear before the conclusion and indicate that it is coming. The most common are *therefore, thus, so, hence, ac-*

cordingly and *consequently*. There are also premise indicator terms that let us know a premise is coming: *since, because, for, in that, seeing that* and *given that*.[4] Many arguments, such as our argument above, do not employ indicator terms. Sometimes you can mentally insert them, and that might help to determine the conclusion. A second tactic is to remember that most of the time the conclusion is either the first or the last sentence in the argument. That is often a good place to start. Sometimes an arguer will place the conclusion somewhere in the middle of the argument, but this usually is not the case. A third tactic is to ask what is the main point of this argument. Try to see the inferential link between the premises and the conclusion. What is the main point the arguer is trying to make? It seems to be that Westminster College is the best small liberal arts college in the state. Everything else seems to be functioning to support that point. That is our conclusion.

Step 2: Rewrite the argument in standard logical order. In order to analyze properly an argument it is helpful to write it out in a form in which the reasoning is apparent. This is where we separate the premises from the conclusion and from each other so we can examine each individual part of the argument. It is common to list the premises first and the conclusion last. In performing this step we have to first ask another question: How many premises are there? You can often organize premises a number of ways. In analyzing our argument, I have had students who organized it into two premises (one about faculty and another about students), three premises (one about faculty and two about students) and four premises (two about faculty and two about students). Which one is correct? While there is not a definitively right answer to this question, we need to remember what our goal is: analysis. In general a good principle when you are analyzing is to break the item down to its smallest parts. Doing so with our argument yields four separate premises. This is also giving the strongest interpretation to the argument, which fulfills another important principle in analysis: give the author of the argument the benefit of interpreting the argument in the strongest way possible. An argument with four reasons in support of the conclusion is

---

[4]There are many more conclusion and premise indicator terms. This is only a sampling.

generally stronger than one with only two. Therefore, our argument can be rewritten:

Faculty are well prepared.
Faculty are professionally active.
Students come in with high scores on college aptitude tests.
Most students are successful in their professions after they graduate.
Therefore, Westminster College is the best small liberal arts college in
   the state.

Step 3: Do these premises support this conclusion? You might ask, "Why is this question next? Shouldn't we first check out the premises and see whether they are true and then see whether they support that conclusion?" There are two reasons why this is the next question. First, remember our goal: we are trying to determine whether we have a good argument or not. At heart, a good argument is one where the conclusion follows from the premises. If the conclusion does not follow, then it does not matter whether the premises are true or not. There is also a practical reason for performing this step now: we can answer this question without doing any extra burdensome work. To check out the truthfulness of each of these premises will involve quite a bit of outside research. However, we can answer the question of inference without even leaving the room. It is right there in front of us. We may have to check out the premises later, but if the conclusion does not follow, then there would be no need—the argument fails. In asking this question first, we assume (for the moment) the premises are true, and we do not worry yet whether they are actually true or not.

Answering this question means we need to look closely at the conclusion and ask ourselves, "What kind of evidence would support this conclusion?" and then see whether that is what is offered. Note that our argument claims that "Westminster College is the best small liberal arts college in the state." It is not saying it is a *good* college, it is saying it is the *best*. There is a big difference. *Best* is a comparative term. It means "in comparison with other small liberal arts colleges." When we look at the evidence being offered, we note that none of it compares *Westminster College* with other small liberal arts colleges. We would expect to see statements like "Their faculty are *better* prepared than faculty at other colleges" or "Students have higher scores than students at other colleges." Instead we get a list of characteristics that might be considered good for a college, but that tells us nothing about Westminster being better than others colleges in these qualities. And that is the claim of the conclusion. Therefore, it looks like our argument, which might at first have appeared to be pretty good, has a fatal flaw—the premises do not support the conclusion. We will continue to use it for practice purposes.

Step 4: Are the premises reliable and true? There are two reasons arguments fail: either the conclusion does not follow from the premises or the premises themselves are not true. If the conclusion follows from the premises, then that means that an argument is valid (in the deductive sense) or strong (in the inductive sense). However, validity or strength is only one part of a successful argument. In order for an argument to succeed, it also needs to be sound or cogent.[5] That requires that we have good reason to believe the premises are in fact true and therefore reliable for reaching the conclusion. When we were analyzing step 3 we assumed the premises were true. Now we need to check that out. This may involve some outside research on our part. Has any evidence been offered that leads me to believe that the faculty are well-prepared and professionally active or that students have received high scores on aptitude tests and are successful in their professions? What kind of evidence would that entail? Most likely we would want to see studies offering us statistics to show that these are in fact true. And if we are going to continue arguing that Westminster College is the best in the state, we are going to want to compare these statistics with statistics from other small liberal arts colleges in the state and see which is superior.

We tend to be reticent in challenging arguers on their evidence, but it is not improper to request such additional supporting evidence. It is not uncommon for arguers to inflate claims to make their evidence sound better than it usually is. Thus, it is quite appropriate to assume that they have these statistics on hand to back up their claims and they should be able to produce them with little effort.

---

[5]You can review these terms in chapter five.

However, we can evaluate the premises on another level that does not require sifting through studies, and that takes us to step 5.

Step 5: Is the language definite and clear? Is there evidence of loaded language? One of the most important lessons I have learned in studying philosophy is the importance of paying attention to the language in which arguments are expressed. We are often subtly manipulated into affirming or rejecting ideas by the language in which those ideas are presented to us. Certain fields, such as advertising and marketing, are expert at employing language to spin an idea in the direction they want the audience to hear or read. Therefore it is extremely important to examine carefully the language in which claims are made to see whether it is accurate, precise and clear.

As we look at the premises and conclusion in our argument, is terminology present that needs clarification and definition? We might want a clear definition of "small liberal arts" college. What criteria are employed to designate which colleges are a member of this group and which are not? How about the terminology in the premises? We might ask what exactly it means for faculty to be well-prepared. Do they all have minimal qualifications that allow them to teach, or do they have advanced and terminal degrees? What is meant by "professionally active"? Do they only teach classes, or are they published in peer-reviewed journals and regularly attend and read papers at conferences in their field? We can ask similar questions about the students. What is a "high score" on a college aptitude test? Is this test, which is an entrance exam, a good measure of the quality of the college, or would a better test be the comprehensive exams taken after they complete their studies at the college? When it is claimed that students are "successful in their professions after they graduate," is the claim being made that they are working in the field in which they are trained, or does it mean they are good at whatever job they got?[6]

The vagueness of these claims leads us to believe this argument probably came from a marketing brochure written to recruit students to Westminster College. Recruiting brochures often intentionally employ vague language in order to make claims that are untestable. If someone

---

[6]It could be claimed that the guy handing out carts at Wal-Mart is also successful in his profession.

claims a university is "the world's most exciting university," what possible means can be devised to test such a claim? The warning here is clear. You should carefully note the language used in an argument and ask, "Is it clear, or do I have questions?"

The next three steps concern three of the most common forms of arguing: arguing by example, arguing by authority and causal arguments.

Step 6: Consider arguing by example. It is common when arguing to use examples as evidence to support your conclusion:

Richard Nixon will go down in history as our most incompetent president. Look at how badly he bungled the Watergate affair. If he had admitted his wrongdoing, he probably would have survived the crisis with little damage.

A number of factors need to be considered when you argue by example. First, you normally cannot arrive at a conclusion on the basis of one example. One example could be atypical, a mere anomaly. In the argument above, it may be that Nixon bungled Watergate but handled most other aspects of his administration extremely well. He was president for almost six years and was involved in a number of policy decisions. To take one instance from his presidency and reach a conclusion is to be guilty of the fallacy of hasty generalization.

A second factor to consider: Are the examples employed representative of the point you are making?

I think we have good reason to believe the conservative Republican candidate will win the presidential election. A poll of Liberty University students on the East coast and the citizens of Orange County, California, on the West coast confirm an overwhelming majority of voters in his favor.

The problem with this example is that while these polls may support the conclusion, the samples polled are known for being predominantly populated with politically conservative individuals. They are hardly representative of the whole country voting for the president. In order for examples to work as evidence they need to be broadly representative.

Another factor to consider in evaluating an argument based on examples is the presence of possible counterexamples. A counterexample is an example that refutes the ones that have been suggested in support of the conclusion. Counterexamples have the function of weakening an argument by showing that the conclusion does not necessarily follow. Note the following:

The Peloponnesian War was caused by the Athenians' desire to dominate Greece. The Napoleonic Wars were caused by Napoleon's desire to dominate Europe. World War II was caused by the fascists' desire also to dominate Europe. Thus all wars are caused by the desire for territorial domination.[7]

The conclusion of this argument is universal: "*All* wars are caused by the desire for territorial domination." If you wanted to challenge this conclusion, you could offer a counterexample by suggesting a war that was not caused by the desire for territorial domination. The American Civil War and the French Revolution would be excellent counterexamples, as they seem to be more about ideas, such as freedom, rights and justice, than about territory. In the earlier example of Richard Nixon, you could point to his foreign policy decisions, which many argue were some of the best of the twentieth century, as counterexamples to the charge of his presidency being the most incompetent. As you can see from these examples, the use of the counterexample method works best when the argument makes universal and extravagant claims.

Step 7: *Consider argument by authority.* None of us is an expert in everything, and so we often have to rely on others to provide information that we may use as evidence in an argument. We call this argument by authority. At least part of the reason why I support a particular conclusion may be that experts who are intimately acquainted with the issue have weighed in and offered their authoritative opinion. Given their expertise, we usually give such testimony a lot of evidential weight. Therefore, if relevant, it is appropriate to quote or cite an expert as support for a position you wish to defend.

Consumer Reports tested the new 2012 model of the Toyota Camry Hybrid LE and found that it gets 43 MPG in the city. Therefore we can conclude that it gets great gas mileage in the city.

---

[7]This example is from Anthony Weston, *A Rulebook for Arguments*, 2nd ed. (Indianapolis: Hackett, 1992), p. 20.

There are a number of factors to consider when arguing by authority. First, it is important that the authority being quoted is a bona fide and informed authority on the issue under consideration. Just because one might be considered an authority in one area does make one an authority in all areas. *Consumer Reports* is a recognized authority in examining and evaluating consumer products. Therefore the argument above is a good one. However, note the following:

All this talk of global warming is nonsense. My pastor spoke on it this past Sunday. He said these kinds of climate fluctuations have been going on for centuries and we have nothing to worry about. He ought to know what he is talking about—he has a graduate degree from one of the top seminaries in the country and has published a number of books.

I have no doubt that this pastor is knowledgeable about a number of areas such as theology and Bible. However, that does not make him an expert on shifting meteorology. A closely related fallacy is individuals who are experts in an adjacent field, but not necessarily an expert on the question under consideration. I recently read a book proposing that the stories of Jesus were taken from ancient Egyptian texts that relate the story of Isis, Osiris and their son Horus. The author quoted as her primary sources experts in Egyptology and Egyptian religion. These authors may have expertise in Egyptian history and religion, but they are not experts on the development of Christian beliefs. The experts in that field almost unanimously refute any claims of a contributing relationship between Jesus and Horus.

Another factor in employing an authority concerns the problem of conflicting authorities. Even authorities often disagree with one another. If you are going to argue by authority, you should attempt to arrive at a consensus of authorities. In many cases this is possible. However, often a consensus is not to be, and it would be disingenuous to claim one. We should avoid claiming a consensus without having done the required research to support such a claim. I have often heard the phrase "the majority of experts say . . ." or "experts say . . ." with little or no evidence offered to support the claim. Similarly it should be noted that merely claiming an expert does not necessarily settle an issue. Authoritative expertise carries a significant amount of weight, but experts can be wrong.

Most philosophers agree that there are some areas where there is not an expert. Ethics, politics and religion are three areas where it is usually recognized that quoting an expert does little to resolve an issue. While there can be experts *about* these topics, it is generally recognized that there are no experts who offer definitive answers on these questions.

Finally, you should remember that *ad hominem* attacks do not discredit an expert. We are valuing the individual's expertise on a specific issue. We are not evaluating his or her personal beliefs, characteristics or actions.

Step 8: Consider causal arguments. We often argue about why an event occurred by pointing back to its cause. For example:

The stock market crash of 1929 was the result of a perfect storm of social and economic events. An agricultural recession along with the speculative bubble of prosperity caused an abnormal increase in debt. These factors coupled with overvalued shares and weakness in the bank system caused the inevitable bubble to burst and the crash to occur.

Arguments like the one above are often found in social, medical, historical and physical sciences. Causal arguments are common, but they can be more complicated than they might initially appear. One factor that will help to strengthen a causal argument is if the argument explains how the cause led to the event. Merely asserting a causal connection is usually not enough to make the argument work and lays you open to the charge of a false cause. You do not need to provide every detail to justify a causal connection, but you should offer some of the elements to show how one event caused another event to occur. In the argument above, enough detail is given to show how the different social and economic elements worked together to cause the 1929 stock market crash.

The above example illustrates another important element in causal arguments. Social events are often the result of multifaceted causes intricately connected together. Rarely is it just one thing, and care needs to be taken to not oversimplify a cause.

SAT scores have dropped to a new low recently. The reason is clear: teachers just aren't doing their jobs anymore.

Although it is tempting to identify one cause for an event and thereby arrive at a supposed quick fix, reality is usually more complicated than that. The reason SAT scores might drop is probably due to a host of factors, one of which *may* be that teachers are not functioning up to speed. This is an oversimplification.

Many events have more than one possible cause. Sometimes it is not so much finding a cause as it is finding the most likely cause for an event. When I was in middle school I heard a story of a ghost that wandered the tracks near where I lived. The story was that many years before a railroad worker fell out of a train and was killed. Now he eternally wanders along the tracks waving his red lantern. One evening some friends and I went to check it out and, sure enough, looking down the tracks we would see a red light suddenly appear and wave across the tracks and then disappear. Now it is broadly possible that the explanation for the effect was the ghost of a railroad worker. However, another explanation was possible. What we were seeing was an intersection further down the tracks where cars drove across the tracks at an angle such that all we could see were their tail lights. It was so far away that we could not hear the cars and could only make out the lights. Which explanation is more likely? It seems without even testing the two that the second explanation is obvious. But why should I automatically say that? When it comes to more than one cause, and we are not able to test them, a good general principle is to embrace the cause that goes with our established beliefs and experiences. As a Christian I am open to supernatural causes for events, but in general I do not jump to a supernatural explanation for a cause unless I have strong evidence that the supernatural is involved.[8]

Finally, it is important that you can show that two events are, in fact, causally connected. Sometimes random events occur that are coincidental and not causally related. Be careful not to jump to conclusions without sufficient evidence that a causal connection is involved, or you might end up affirming an argument like the following:

Bread is bad for you. Why? Consider the following facts: More than 98 percent of convicted felons are bread users. Half of all children who grow

[8]One important factor would be that the event occurs in a supernatural environment, such as in answer to prayer.

up in bread-consuming households score below average on standardized tests. In the eighteenth century, a time when bread was baked primarily in homes, life expectancy was less than fifty, and infant mortality rates were high. More than 90 percent of violent crimes take place within twenty-four hours of eating bread. The conclusion is obvious: Stop eating bread.

Step 9: *Check for fallacies.* The final step in evaluating an argument is to look for any formal or informal fallacies within the argument. This requires that you have a good understanding of logic and of the informal fallacies we discussed in the previous chapter. In general the main thing you are looking for is a *non sequitur*. Does the conclusion follow from the premise? If not, identify the fallacy being committed. This is not easy and takes practice. However, if you work hard at it you can become an expert analyst. By doing so, you will live a fuller and richer life and will become a more effective disciple of Jesus Christ.

EPILOGUE

Seven Virtues of a Christian Philosopher

I would be remiss if I were to write a book introducing philosophy to Christians and did not take some space to discuss those qualities that I believe make one a good Christian philosopher. Philosophy is about more than examining and evaluating arguments or gaining knowledge about abstract concepts. In the first chapter I contrasted a job with an occupational vocation and stated that philosophy is more like the latter. Developing the philosophical mindset is a way of life, a process of becoming a particular kind of person. Perhaps the best way to express this is in the language of virtues.

The concept of virtue has a long and honored tradition in Western philosophy. From the beginning many philosophers recognized that our actions and the activities we pursue are largely dependent on the character qualities that are embedded into us from the earliest days of our childhood. These character qualities are called virtues and vices. A virtue is a trained behavioral disposition to act in a good or righteous manner, and a vice is its opposite. Virtues and vices are analogous to good and bad habits. If you think of a habit, it is something that is built into your personality through practice over time such that you may rarely think of it but regularly act on it. Virtues are honorable characteristics that become a part of who we are. They are often so much a part of our being and personality that we may be associated with them: "He is a man of integrity." Traditionally virtues have been divided into two categories: moral virtues, such as kindness, humility or honesty; and intellectual virtues, such as wisdom, studiousness or inquisitiveness. Although there is no one definitive list of virtues, historically a set of moral virtues developed over time that came to be known as the seven cardinal virtues: prudence, temperance, fortitude, justice, faith, hope and love. It was believed that all other virtues flowed from these seven.

In like manner, I want to propose seven virtues of a Christian philosopher. As I do so, let me first note that virtues do not stand in isolation. They are teleological and communal. By teleological we mean that they have a goal or purpose. Aristotle suggested that the goal for the virtues was the achievement of *eudaimonia*, or the good life. By communal, we mean that the virtues are formed within a community of individuals with a shared conception of what that good life is. Christians form such a community, and I would like to suggest that the ultimate goal for Christians in general, and for Christian philosophers in particular, is to glorify God. The Westminster Larger Catechism says it best: "Man's chief end is to glorify God and to enjoy him forever."[1] Therefore the virtues of the Christian philosopher are those that glorify God. What might these be?

Love of truth. Christian philosophers have an unquenchable love of the truth. It is this love of truth that drives an undying intellectual curiosity to know and understand the deep things of God and of his creation. This appetite for truth is insatiable: the more we know, the more we desire to know. The more educated we become, the more we realize how little we know, and hence the appetite continues to grow. We read, reflect, discuss and read more in an effort to understand.[2]

Like any virtue, an excess of the desire to know can become the vice of vicious curiosity, where our desire to know so controls us that we neglect other moral and epistemic duties. The history of medical research is littered with stories of abuses by well-meaning researchers who trampled on the rights and values of individuals in their quest for

[1] Westminster Larger Catechism (1648), question 1.
[2] That is why philosophers often own so many books.

knowledge. However, of greater concern is the opposite vice that has become rampant in modern Christian evangelicalism: anti-intellectualism. Some are almost proud of their lack of knowledge. Such an attitude does not bring glory to God, for people are not loving the Lord with their minds when they refuse to use that mind to the best of their ability. Os Guinness writes,

At root, evangelical anti-intellectualism is both a scandal and a sin. It is a scandal in the sense of being an offense and a stumbling block that needlessly hinders serious people from considering the Christian faith and coming to Christ. It is a sin because it is a refusal, contrary to the first of Jesus' two great commandments, to love the Lord our God with our minds. Anti-intellectualism is quite simply a sin. Evangelicals must address it as such, beyond all excuses, evasions, or rationalizations of false piety.[3]

The reasons for this spirit of anti-intellectualism are varied: laziness, bad theology and bad exegesis are some. Many Christians are afraid of the truth. They fear that it will hinder their faith and cause doubt. However, God is the author of all truth, and all truth is God's truth. If your faith is not true, then why believe it? And if it is true, then there is no fear in questioning and examining it. Christian philosophers embrace the search for truth.

Diligence. There is no denying that philosophy is hard work. It often takes many hours of reading and reflecting on complex ideas. It takes a significant amount of effort to construct an argument or to understand the structure of a problem. I often find that after a few hours of reading and writing about a difficult philosophical work that I am as tired as if I had been digging a trench in my backyard. So the virtue of diligence is necessary in order to push through and do the work that philosophical thinking requires. Diligence is the idea of persistent and continuous industry to accomplish a task. It is the virtue of not quitting, even, and especially, when the desire to quit is overwhelming. The opposite vice is laziness. We live in a day where we are regularly tempted to do only what minimally needs to be done. I often see this in classes. Many stu-

[3]Os Guinness, *Fit Bodies, Fat Minds: Why Evangelicals Don't Think and What to Do About It* (Grand Rapids: Baker, 1994), pp. 10-11.

dents are concerned more with getting a grade than with getting an education. Such a minimal goal provides fertile ground for a "doing the least I can do to get by" attitude. Because Christian philosophers love truth, they are willing to do the hard work necessary to obtain it; hence the need for diligence.

Intellectual honesty. In his book on virtue epistemology, Jay Wood says, "Like so much of the virtuous life, seeking truth appropriately is a matter of seeking in the right way, for the right reason, using for the right methods and for the right purposes."[4] It would not make sense to strive to find the truth in order to glorify God and to do so dishonestly. Honesty involves the means and methods we employ in our search, as well as the results. Many of us passionately hold on to our beliefs with firm commitments. Such passion might tempt us to skew our research and evidence in favor of the direction we want it to go, rather than letting it point us in the direction of what is true. It was Antony Flew's lifelong motto of "following the evidence wherever it leads" that led to his conversion to theism late in life.

It is easy to be blinded by our commitments and lose sight of our goal of finding the truth. However, any view that is arrived at through dishonest means is not going to provide us with truth and is not honoring to God, no matter how much we think it might be. I have seen good, intelligent people become so blinded as to use dishonest means to obtain what they sincerely believe is true. I once listened to a lecture by a Christian scientist. He related a story about visiting a museum that had shown a short film about evolution. The scientist noted what he thought were a number of serious problems in the presentation and asked to purchase a copy of the film to show his students. The museum staff explained that the film was not available for purchase or reproduction. The scientist then told us how he took his camcorder into the museum theater and illegally videotaped a copy of the film that he regularly shows in class. His zeal to teach the truth blinded him to the immoral and illegal actions he performed. God is not glorified when we attempt to teach truth through deception. We live in a culture in which the

[4]W. Jay Wood, *Epistemology: Becoming Intellectually Virtuous* (Downers Grove, IL: InterVarsity Press, 1998), p. 57.

maxim "it's easier to get forgiveness than permission" has become the new standard for morality. Christian philosophers are honest in how they obtain their data and honestly report the data they obtain.

Fairness and respect. Christian philosophers treat others fairly and with respect. This virtue is in short supply among many Christians today. We live in a world of partisan politics where a white hat/black hat mentally has become all too pervasive. We demonize anyone who is not on our side of an issue. All who claim to be Christians are our friends and supporters, and all who claim otherwise are "the enemy." Many are deluded into thinking that our friends can say and do no wrong and the enemy can say and do no right. Christian philosophers are acutely aware that this is not an accurate reflection of reality and is an attitude that does not glorify God. Those who hold beliefs that are different from ours and argue for those beliefs are not the enemy. Many of them are philosophers and thinkers who, like us, are on a journey to discover the truth. We might disagree, but we can still respect them for the work they do and treat them in a fair and equitable manner. Christian philosophers do not have a problem with disagreement. They mutually respect men and women of all beliefs and ideas. In fact, many of my friends are individuals (both Christians and non-Christians) with whom I disagree on a number of issues. Yet I respect them because they are good thinkers.

Intellectual fortitude. Fortitude is a kind of courage, but it is different from bravery. Fortitude is the virtue that supports us when we need to overcome obstacles that arise in our journey. Think of the people who settled the West. They knew they would encounter incredible difficulties along the way: forging raging rivers, crossing endless deserts and scaling the tallest peaks. One can imagine the fear they faced as they set out on the journey. Fortitude is what got them through. Fortitude is not the absence of fear. It is working through our fears to achieve a goal. Christian philosophers often face a difficult journey, especially in a day when secularism and naturalism dominate our institutions of higher learning. They know that the beliefs they often defend are not popular in academia. The pressure to give in or to back off on one's beliefs can be enormous. Intellectual fortitude is a necessary virtue to maintain the faith in increasing opposition, for it is not easy to promote an unpopular view. I recently observed a Christian thinker suggest a view that was unpopular among many Christians. Though he knew it would be unpopular, he believes he is right and produced good arguments for the view. It was fascinating to observe as he faced tremendous hostility and resistance from many, some of whom claimed to be his friends and allies. He lost his job, his reputation suffered, and many speaking engagements were rescinded because of the unpopular position he took. It would have been easy for him to recant his view. But he believes he is right. Whether he is or not, I admire his intellectual fortitude in standing by his principles. Such fortitude glorifies God.

Epistemic humility. Epistemic humility is the virtue of recognizing that we are limited in our knowledge and in our ability to know. Recognizing this limitation is a key to growing and learning. In a desire to convey confidence in their beliefs, many Christians make claims that go far beyond what the evidence allows. They become arrogant and proud in their delusion of how much they think they know. They need to recognize that most problems are more complex than they assume and that many intelligent and sincere people whose views differ from their own offer very good arguments in support of those views. Epistemically humble Christian philosophers offer arguments unpretentiously, recognizing their own fallibility, and are open to being shown where they might be wrong in their reasoning. They know the difference between views of which they can be confident and those they hold with reservation. Above all, they know the difference between confidence and arrogance and avoid the latter. When they encounter views of those with whom they disagree, they listen respectfully and seek to understand. They look for areas of commonality and respectfully note differences of opinion.

The need for epistemic humility brings up a special group worth commenting on: the novice philosopher. In the thirty years that I have been teaching philosophy, I have noticed how we philosophy teachers are in constant danger of creating philosophical Frankensteins: students who pick up a little philosophy, perhaps taking a course or two, and become arrogant, elitist little monsters. I have observed the haughty attitudes of these students toward their fellow students who do not understand the wealth of knowledge *they* have obtained. I am reminded of what one of my professors told me many years ago: the more you understand a subject, the more humble you become as you realize how enormous it is and how little you are. First Corinthians 8:1 (KJV) says, "Knowledge puffeth up." I would remind my novice students to maintain epistemic humility and to remember that they are not that far from where their fellow students are. We are all on this journey together. None of us has the right to think we have arrived.

Teachableness. The last virtue follows nicely on the tail of epistemic humility. Good Christian philosophers are teachable. They are open to learning from others. This involves all of the former virtues. To be teachable means that, out of love for truth, you are willing to place yourself under the guidance of another, which involves epistemic humility. It is to honestly admit a certain amount of ignorance, which takes courage, and to be willing to listen and to learn, even from those with whom we might find some disagreement, which takes respect. It involves hard work in understanding and communicating with the teacher, which takes diligence. Jesus looked for disciples who were teachable. The Christian philosopher needs to model this virtue.

You might say, "Yes, this is all well and good. But I am not going to be a philosopher by trade. I have another vocation in mind." If you think that, then you have missed the point of this book, for all Christians are called to be philosophers. Developing the philosophical mindset is one of the most important ways we understand God and his world. Through this he is glorified. *Soli gloria Deo.*

ANSWERS TO EXERCISES

CHAPTER FIVE

1. Deductive, categorical syllogism, invalid. The reason this syllogism is invalid is that it breaks the first rule for a categorical syllogism (p. 128), which states that the middle term must be distributed at least once in the premises. In this case the middle term is "students who understand logic," and it is undistributed both times it appears. Since only some of the students who understand logic will get an A, there is no guarantee Lisa will get one.

2. Inductive, generalization, strong. Generally, if a person wears big shoes and his feet sink an inch into dry ground, then he is going to be a heavy man. If he bumps his head on the rafters, he will be tall as well. While none of this is necessarily true, it is probably the case. That is all you need for the argument to be strong.

3. Deductive, hypothetical syllogism, valid. This is the *modus ponens* version of the hypothetical syllogism which states that, if that antecedent (the "if" part) is true, then the consequent (the "then" part) must follow. You might have been thrown off by the claim of the first premise, but remember that the argument is valid if the conclusion follows from the premises no matter what those premises claim.

4. Deductive, disjunctive syllogism, valid. Disjunctive syllogisms are just presenting a process of elimination. If the first premise is providing us with only two options and one of them did not occur, then the other must have occurred, assuming both premises are true.

5. Inductive, analogy, strong. If the two types of tiles are relevantly similar, than what is true of one is probably true of the other.

6. Inductive, prediction, weak. The wishful thinking that hopes "the Lions can't keep losing forever" is not enough evidence to argue against the win/loss record of both teams. Given that record, the chances are likely that Green Bay will beat the Lions.

7. Deductive, hypothetical syllogism, invalid. In a valid hypothetical syllogism the second premise can either affirm the antecedent or deny the consequent. However, this syllogism denied the antecedent. That is the fallacy. The first premise only tells us that if deism is true, then the Bible is false. But it doesn't say anything about what happens if deism is false. It may be that the Bible is true, but you can't arrive at that conclusion through this argument.

8. Inductive, causal inference, weak. Without providing any more evidence, there is no reason to believe that the neighbor's teenager poured sugar into the gas tank. More likely, the battery was dead, as that is the most common reasons cars do not start in freezing cold temperatures.

9. Deductive, categorical syllogism, valid. Remember that valid only means that the conclusion follows from the premises. If the two premises are assumed to be true, then the conclusion follows and Toby has good artistic talent.

10. Deductive, hypothetical syllogism, valid. While the truthfulness of both of these premises is debated by philosophers, the argument is valid because the conclusion follows if we assume they are true. This is a classic argument for God's existence.

11. Inductive, argument based on authority, weak. Remember that for an argument based on authority to be strong, the authority must be an expert in the area under discussion. The fact that Dr. Jones is an expert in physics does not qualify him as an authority on psychic phenomena.

12. Inductive, statistical reasoning, strong. The poll conducted was with a large number of college students and was representative across a variety of college campuses scattered throughout the country. Therefore the chances are likely that the conclusion is correct assuming the premises are true.

13. Deductive, disjunctive syllogism, invalid. Since the idea behind the disjunctive syllogism is a process of elimination, this syllogism is invalid. The elimination must occur in the second premise, not in the conclusion. Because disjunctives are interpreted as being in-

clusive, the first premise allows for the fact that both Phyllis and Stuart could attend the conference. So knowing one went does not tell me the other did not.

14. Deductive, hypothetical syllogism, invalid. While it is true that the syllogism does not commit the fallacy of affirming the consequent, it does commit the fallacy of denying the antecedent. Thus it is invalid. To deny the antecedent doesn't mean the consequent cannot occur. If I say "If you cut off my head, then I will die," and I never get my head cut off, it does not mean I will never die.

15. Inductive, generalization, strong. If most of the students at Liberty University are Christians, and Kelly is a student there, then it is more likely that Kelly is in the majority rather than the minority. Remember, strong doesn't mean it is certain, it just means that it is more probable than not.

CHAPTER SIX

1. False cause. It is very weak to argue that Boggs's practice of eating chicken and taking batting practice at a specific time was the cause of his success as a ball player.

2. Weak analogy. While human beings and computers have some similarities, they are not relevantly similar when it comes to the basis for human rights.

3. Slippery slope. Notice the step-by-step progression to the extreme conclusion. However, there is no reason to believe that simply reexamining assessment policies will lead to such a grim and extreme outcome.

4. Hasty generalization. It seems that three cases are too small and unrepresentative a group to make any conclusion about each and every student.

5. Sweeping generalization. While it is true that the Constitution generally guarantees free speech, there are limits to that freedom, as there are to all our freedoms. You cannot use your freedom to put other lives in danger.

6. Composition. There is certainly more to the "Gettysburg Address" than just the individual words.

7. Hypostatization. Greed is an abstract concept and does not have the ability to build, improve or do a job.

8. Division. What is true of the whole jury may not be true of any particular individual member. The decision of whole corporately together may not reflect the thinking of Erin herself.

9. Amphiboly. The question concerns how we should interpret the phrase "picture of Jeannette hidden in his locker." Is it referring to a picture that he is hiding in his locker and the picture is of Jeannette? Or does it mean that Jeannette was hiding in Paul's locker and he got a picture of her while in there? It is not clear.

10. Equivocation. The fallacy is that the term *miracle* is being used in two different ways. When speaking of the "miracles of the Bible," the speaker is being quite literal and thinking of a miracle as a divine supernatural event that interrupts the normal course of natural events. However, when he speaks of the "miracle of birth," he is using the term in a metaphorical sense. Birth is a normal and natural event that occurs through the regular process of biological reproduction. It may be a joyous and wondrous event, but it is not a divine intervention interrupting the normal course of natural events.

11. Special pleading. This individual has a real problem with her sister going through her things, but seems to think, without any justification, that there is nothing wrong in doing the same to her.

12. Begging the question. This is the circular version of the fallacy. In answering the question of why philosophy instructors are intelligent, he simply says "Because they are." The reason and the conclusion are saying the same thing.

13. Complex question. There are really two questions involved here: "Have you been cheating?" and "How long have you been cheating?" The individual being asked is not given the opportunity to answer the first question.

14. Bifurcation. Only two options are being offered here when more are possible. For example, it could simply be that she is mistaken or is being misunderstood.

15. Special pleading. Notice in this example how the language masks the fallacy. When speaking of ourselves we speak euphemistically of "stocking up." When speaking of the others we speak pejoratively: they are "hoarding." One wonders if there is really much of a difference between what we are doing and what they are doing.

16. Ad hominem. This is the circumstantial form of the fallacy. The idea is that, since Fox may personally benefit from stem cell research, we should disregard his arguments. However, the fact that a person might benefit from what they are arguing for has no bearing on whether they have a good argument or not. The strength of the argument itself has nothing to do with the motives behind why one argues for a particular position.

17. Red herring. Notice how the arguer subtly changed the subject from being about academics to being about the way students behave. He never actually addressed the problem his opponent raised.

18. Appeal to pity. While one can certainly sympathize with Steve's plight, the award is for the best essay, and it would be unfair to give him the award for an inferior essay on the basis of feeling sorry for him.

19. Straw man. The problem is that the workers never argued for an expensive new air-conditioning system. They just wanted to improve the ventilation. In the classic straw man tactic, their request was taken to an extreme position that was then torn down with the respondent assuming he addressed the original argument when he had not.

20. Ad populum. The point being made is that one should accept evolution as true merely because it is popular. However, one should evaluate evolution on the strength of the evidence, not on the number of people who believe in it—no matter how much of their brain is involved.

Index